Alan Butler qualified as an engineer, but has spent the last 30 years immersed in the history of the world and developing an expertise in ancient cosmology and astronomy. He has created many books, the majority of which delve into the recesses of the past that often remain ignored. Under his own name he has published books such as *The Virgin and the Pentacle*, *Sheep,* and *How to Read Prehistoric Monuments.* Together with Christopher Knight he has co-authored four books, and other co-operative ventures include the acclaimed *Rosslyn Revealed* with John Ritchie.

In addition to writing books Alan is an accomplished playwright and has written many plays for the stage and a number for national radio. He lives on the North Yorkshire coast of England with his wife Kate and when not pounding away at the computer or travelling he is to be found in his workshop, building musical instruments or tinkering with his ancient sports car.

Other books by Alan Butler

The Bronze Age Computer Disc
The Warrior and the Bankers
The Templar Continuum
The Goddess, the Grail and the Lodge
The Virgin and the Pentacle
Sheep
How to Read Prehistoric Monuments

By Alan Butler and Christopher Knight
Before the Pyramids
Civilization One
Who Built the Moon?
Solomon's Power Brokers

By Alan Butler and John Ritchie
Rosslyn Revisited

CITY OF THE GODDESS

FREEMASONS, THE SACRED FEMININE, AND THE SECRET BENEATH THE SEAT OF POWER IN
WASHINGTON, DC

ALAN BUTLER

WATKINS PUBLISHING
LONDON

This edition first published in the UK and USA 2011 by
Watkins Publishing, Sixth Floor, Castle House,
75–76 Wells Street, London W1T 3QH

1 3 5 7 9 10 8 6 4 2

Designed and typeset by Jerry Goldie Graphic Design

Printed and bound in China by Imago

British Library Cataloguing-in-Publication Data Available

Library of Congress Cataloging-in-Publication Data Available

ISBN: 978-1-78028-029-5

www.watkinspublishing.co.uk

Distributed in the USA and Canada by Sterling Publishing Co., Inc.
387 Park Avenue South, New York, NY 10016-8810

For information about custom editions, special sales, premium and
corporate purchases, please contact Sterling Special Sales
Department at 800-805-5489 or specialsales@sterlingpub.com

This book is humbly dedicated to Washington DC, one of the most beautiful, inspiring and enigmatic cities in the world and also to the memory of Thomas Jefferson, who in my opinion was more responsible for its creation than any other person.

CONTENTS

List of Plates

1. The Washington Monument; phallic expression of both God and Goddess.

2. A view from the middle of the Lincoln Memorial on the Mall.

3. One of the speeches carved into the wall of the Jefferson Memorial.

4–8. Some of the many goddesses to be seen on statues and monuments around Washington DC.

9. The exact spot that marks the very centre of Washington DC Ellipse Park.

10. The United States distance marker stone.

11. The security helicopter that remained overhead for the whole time we were examining the centre of Ellipse Park.

12. The centre of Ellipse Park looking south along the prime meridian towards the Jefferson Memorial.

13. A view down Pennsylvania Avenue towards the Capitol.

14. Part of the World War II Memorial on the Mall.

15. The White House north front, looking south from Lafayette Square down the old prime meridian.

16. Lafayette Square, immediately to the north of the White House.

17. Christopher Knight and Alan Butler in Ellipse Park, Washington DC.

18. The easternmost marker stone for the District of Columbia.

19. The Capitol, Washington DC, surmounted by the Goddess of Freedom.

20. A map of the streets of central Washington DC including the Megalithic connections between squares and intersections.

21. The Pentagon – the most significant building in Washington DC in terms of its Megalithic credentials.

22. Masonic symbols placed by architect John Wood on the buildings in Kings Circus, Bath, England.

23. The meridian marker stone set in the ground, just below the turf at the very centre of Ellipse Park in Washington DC.

INTRODUCTION

At the start of the second decade of the 21st century Washington DC is the most powerful and influential city in the world. As capital of the world's major remaining superpower, not only is Washington DC the bastion of the United States government and legal system, it also houses the headquarters of the most awesome military machine ever to exist on our planet. Behind the many doors of Washington offices, and especially those in the White House, decisions are taken that have a pronounced bearing on people living thousands of miles away. Since the end of the Second World War, the fate of many nations has been decided in the stately buildings along its elegant tree-lined avenues. During the long and complicated history of our species, no place has been more important or more influential than Washington DC.

All of this we know, and more or less take for granted. True, the position of the United States in world affairs isn't supported by everyone – far from it, and as a result, on almost any weekend of the year large demonstrations march along the Mall in Washington or gather in Lafayette Park, close to the White House.

Walk through the centre of Washington DC and you will come across people of all nationalities, colours and political affiliations. This is a city that is far more cosmopolitan than Rome ever was, more significant than Athens and more stunning in its architecture than many cities that are older by centuries. Part of the reason for its architectural beauty lies in the fact that it never *evolved,* as other cities did, across the centuries. Rather it was planned and built to be exactly what it is. No expense was spared and its planners were at liberty to do more or less what they wished.

Washington DC lies at the heart of a generally Christian nation. True, the United States has citizens from a broad cross-section of beliefs but, generally speaking, America revolves around the same Christianity that many of its first European settlers brought with them to the New World. But despite this, and the number of churches to be found on its streets, Washington DC is not a Christian city, nor was it built to celebrate any of the beliefs held sacred by any of the major religions of the modern world.

At the very creation of the American Constitution a deliberate decision was made to put a fundamental gap between the religious beliefs and practices of individuals and the way the state would be run. Those who founded the United States and Washington DC made it very clear how they felt about allowing religion to get in the way of democratic government. There was no apparent ambiguity to their intentions. If you are ever in Washington DC, take a walk or a cab to the Jefferson Memorial; there, chiselled deep into the wall alongside the statue of Thomas Jefferson, probably the most important and certainly the most literate of the founding fathers, you can read these words that Jefferson himself spoke:

> No man shall be compelled to frequent or support any
> religious worship or ministry or shall otherwise suffer on
> account of his religious opinions or belief, but all men
> shall be free to profess and by argument to maintain, their
> opinions in matters of religion. I know but one code of
> morality for men whether acting singly or collectively.

This sentiment is enshrined in the law of the United States. Most people are familiar with the United States motto, 'In God we Trust', but few realize that it first appeared only in 1864, nearly a century after the foundation of the

United States and, even then, that it came about as a result of a Christian resurgence after the terrible tragedy and loss of life that was the American Civil War. Prior to this, the infant United States used *E pluribus unum*, which means, 'Out of many, one'. At first sight this motto, which appeared on the Great Seal of the United States, has no religious overtones and was taken (of all things) from an ancient Greek poem about a peasant making a salad for his breakfast!

Not that the founding fathers of the United States were necessarily godless. Many were practising Christians, while others, in deference to the Age of Reason in which they were living, would doubtless have described themselves as 'Deists' – they believed in a Creator but did not care to be more specific – or else they refused to be drawn on their true beliefs. What is particularly interesting is that at the very start of the free American adventure, with the Declaration of Independence, the Deity *is* mentioned in the first sentence, but no gender or religious affiliation appears.

> We hold these truths to be self-evident, that all men are created equal, that they are endowed by their Creator with certain unalienable Rights, that among these are Life, Liberty and the pursuit of Happiness.

If most of those who led the American War of Independence against their British overlords were from apparently Christian backgrounds, why did they go to such great lengths to exclude Christianity from the foundation of their new nation? This is an interesting question and it probably has many answers. Some would say it was a reaction to the same oppression that originally forced so many people to travel to the New World – from Catholic or Protestant versions of Christianity that were intolerant of Christian sects that did not accord with their own beliefs. Others might comment that early American nationalists had been much influenced by their French counterparts and suggest that the anti-religious feeling that would later inspire the French Revolution carried across the Atlantic to America.

Many commentators place the reason for the insistence on an apparently secular state as lying within the Craft of Freemasonry. There is no doubt that many of those who led the American colonies to war against Britain and who ultimately became the leaders of the new nation were practising Freemasons. Freemasonry itself was very careful when it came to its declarations regarding religious belief. The only religious prerequisite for admission to most forms of Freemasonry is a belief in a Creator. Who or what the Creator might be is not specified and, in most cases, this unknown progenitor is referred to as either 'The Great Architect' or 'The Grand Geometrician'; terms through which neither religious affiliation nor gender are specified.

There is no doubt that Freemasonry played an important part in the foundation of the United States and the creation of Washington DC, though I have also learned that Freemasonry is a *part* of the story and it is not the whole tale by any means. Some years ago I wrote a book called *The Goddess, the Grail and the Lodge*.[1] While researching this particular book I began to understand just how important the slightly strange rituals and beliefs of Freemasons had been to the creation of the United States, but I came across other factors, and one in particular, that were also highly significant. These were related to Freemasonry but not dependent upon it.

Only within the last couple of years did I begin to truly understand why the founding fathers of the United States acted in the way they did, regarding religion. They were not simply protecting the state from religious interference – they were also carefully protecting themselves.

Last year my friend Christopher Knight and I were writing a book about the very earliest measuring systems used by our ancient ancestors. The book dealt mainly with the Atlantic seaboard of Europe and with ancient Egypt, but we suddenly found ourselves, by the strangest set of circumstances, looking at the United States and Washington DC in particular.[2] What we discovered there not only confirmed our common suspicions regarding Freemasonry, but also supported my own previous evidence regarding the survival of a religious imperative that was literally thousands of years old.

One of the main reasons the founding fathers of the free United States wanted nothing to do with Christianity, at least as far as the state was concerned, was that a fair proportion of them believed in something radically different to Christianity, Judaism, Islam or any of the predominant world religions of the time. Instead they held to a belief in a female deity and in a form of mystery religion that, according to history, disappeared at least 1,600 years ago. I appreciate that this is a massive statement, but I hope that what follows will prove that this was the case. I also intend to show that, as far as a sizeable number of powerbrokers in the United States are concerned, the belief in a perpetual, matriarchal force remains not only significant but imperative.

As for Freemasonry, it is now quite a few years since I first began to realize what lay at the heart of the Craft. No matter what Freemasons say or believe to the contrary, I hope that the evidence I present throughout this book will prove that Freemasonry is a hangover from the ancient mystery religions of Demeter and Isis. The majority of Freemasons alive today are ignorant of this and might laugh at the very suggestion.

This is not to suggest that the answers to the puzzles regarding the planning and creation of Washington DC are to be found exclusively within Freemasonry. If we take an example from the Christian Church we might look at the Jesuits, a Roman Catholic brotherhood founded in 1540. The Jesuits were part of the intellectual heart of Catholicism and have been extremely important as teachers, missionaries, scholars and experts in Christian theology. All Jesuits are Catholics, but not all Catholics are Jesuits. Similarly, all Freemasons are Goddess worshippers (whether or

...ot they realize it) but not all Goddess worshippers are Freemasons. As an example I could mention Thomas Jefferson again. In his personal beliefs, Jefferson was deeply wedded to the concept of the perpetual Goddess, but as far as we can tell he was never a Freemason.

Part of the answer to the planning and creation of Washington DC is to be found in the sky above our heads. One aspect of the personal beliefs of those who had the most influence over the concept of Washington DC was that elements of the starry sky were deeply significant. In this they betray a truly ancient pedigree to their beliefs and, as we shall see, Washington DC was planned and orientated specifically with the signs of the zodiac, and one sign in particular, in mind.

Washington DC is also built on a grid or pattern that cannot be seen with the naked eye. Unlike some other researchers I do not manipulate the gridiron nature of Washington DC's streets to concoct satanic symbols that were supposedly put there for some reason. Our discoveries show that the real matrix upon which Washington DC was created is subtle but irrefutable, and it relates to the same mathematical and geometrical knowledge that went into the creation of structures such as Stonehenge during the late Stone Age and Bronze Age. It is part of a pattern that, many years ago, I named 'The Web of Demeter', and it is at least as old as the European Stone Age.

The plan for Washington DC is part of a mathematical legacy that flourished up to 5,500 years ago, during the high point of matriarchal religion, but which ceased to be used openly by the time that patriarchies began to predominate. This system of geometry and mathematics had already fallen into disuse and been forgotten long before the ancient Greeks were even born; it flourished over a thousand years before the first pyramid was built in Egypt and yet it stands at the very heart of the building of many of Washington DC's most iconic structures. If this sounds unlikely or absurd, I hope to demonstrate that it is nevertheless true.

Washington DC is replete with symbolism, deliberately put there to foster a way of looking at the world that seems strange in the light of more modern religious beliefs. It, and the very district of which it is the central part, was created with these symbols deliberately placed at its heart. To modern sensibilities some of these symbols may seem quite shocking. In the pages that follow, the reader will come across references to sacred vaginas and phallic structures. But times change and doubtless some of the sentiments and beliefs we hold as relevant or even sacred today would have seemed equally shocking to our ancient ancestors.

Those of a radical religious persuasion might use what follows as a means to try to bolster their own beliefs that Washington DC is nothing less than the 'harlot of Babylon' and that it lies at the centre of a diabolic plan to rule the world. I cannot argue with the last suggestion because Washington DC has not merely *planned* to rule the world but has also achieved such an objective to a great extent. However, as to the supposedly diabolic nature of the beliefs that went into creating Washington DC, it has always been the way of religions to consider others' gods to be devils. Religion is a jealous master, as those who created the United States and Washington DC knew only too well. I would also go so far as to suggest that the great secret of Washington DC may be suspected or even well understood in certain places – for example in the darkened corridors of the Vatican. Of all the world's faiths, history shows that Christianity has exhibited the least tolerance of all. No wonder then that the true nature of Washington DC had to be kept a closely guarded secret.

The reader will discover that the size, shape, nature and positioning of structures placed in specific locations in Washington DC, even within the last decade, show that the imperatives and intentions of those who first planned the city are alive and well. This must mean that the belief pattern underpinning them is also still in existence. Since not just anyone can decide where to place a building, it stands to reason that recognition of the Goddess and her mysteries still exists amongst those who are at the very centre of decision-making in the United States. What this means for our future is open to speculation because, after all, the secret is still being kept in Washington DC.

I have no personal axe to grind regarding any of the material in this book. Despite being invited to do so I have resisted calls to become a Freemason, not because I have anything against the Craft, but mainly because I felt I could not speak what I see to be the truth regarding Freemasonry if I were to be restricted by its oaths, which I would feel honour bound to uphold.

Neither do I hold to any specific creed or religion that would inhibit my research or cause me to take sides in what has been a spiritual battle, albeit one that has raged in apparent silence, for so long.

What lies ahead in this book is a truly awe-inspiring journey. It will take us back to a period long before known history began, to the Holy Land, the vineyards of northern France and to a series of remote and little understood prehistoric structures in Britain. We will visit ancient Greece and that most enigmatic civilization in Egypt all so that we can better understand the motivations that went into planning and building Washington DC.

What follows would be the stuff of novels were it not for the fact that, at every turn, there is more than enough evidence to show what has been taking place, right under our noses, for so long. To repeat a phrase Chris Knight and I have used before, 'The world is truly not what we thought it was.'

As if the truth about Washington DC and its creation is not extraordinary enough, at its very centre is something truly astounding. There is a treasure in Washington DC that would make the tomb of Tutankhamen seem as nothing by comparison. It is a treasure that involves all of us because it can tell us so much about our past, and almost certainly inform the ultimate future of humanity.

Alan Butler, Bridlington, England

CHAPTER ONE

AN AIR OF MYSTERY

A City Built on Ancient and Astronomical Principles

Wednesday 18 September, 1793, marked a watershed in the life of the new United States of America. Before this date the United States existed mainly on paper, through the Declaration of Independence of 1776, a document reinforced by the later Constitution signed in 1787.

Shortly before the middle of the day on that Wednesday in 1793, a great procession passed along the muddy tracks on the south side of the Potomac River. At the head of the procession, and indeed at its middle and its rear, were virtual battalions of Freemasons, from two different lodges. This was a civil ceremony, undertaken on behalf of all the citizens of the free United States, but there wasn't any doubt about who was in charge of it.

The procession, led by free America's first president, George Washington, was headed for the hill at the east end of what would one day be the Mall, to a place where land had been cleared for the building of the Capitol, the very centre of US democracy and a symbol of freedom from oppression and the right to self-determination. True, the United States had functioned as a free state for some time, ever since November 1782 when, in Paris, the British effectively admitted they had been beaten militarily and ceded all American territory between the Appalachian Mountains and the Mississippi River to the free United States. But all the meetings that had taken place since then, to enact laws and make suggestions for the new republic, had been stopgaps. They were not held in buildings specifically sanctioned for the purpose and took place in locations that could not be considered neutral to the early states of the republic, some of which were ready to fall out with each other at the drop of a hat.

With the completion of the Capitol, the United States would have a custom-built parliament building to rival any on the planet. What is more, it would stand at the heart of a city that occupied land in *no* specific state and which existed entirely because of the willingness of all the component parts of the United States to co-operate for the federal good.

The President and his entourage crossed the Potomac River and proceeded to President's Square. There they were met by even more Freemasons and, with the President at their head, they processed up to the site of the Capitol. There, with due deference, speeches and prayers, George Washington, himself a leading Freemason, ceremonially laid the cornerstone of the Capitol. The purpose of the whole Washington DC adventure was on its way to completion.

Not only was President Washington surrounded by at least four assembled lodges of Freemasons as he stepped forward and took hold of the ceremonial trowel, but he acknowledged the fact by wearing the lambskin apron that announced his own rank as a Master Mason of the Third Degree. The ceremony was inspired by the Craft because cornerstones have always had a special part to play in Freemasonic symbolism. The cornerstone laid that day in the northeast corner of the Capitol represented the cornerstone of Solomon's Temple in far-off Jerusalem, a building that stands at the very centre of Freemasonic belief and practice. The physical temple (in this case the Capitol) was said to be a metaphor for the spiritual temple that lies within each Freemason's heart, and the cornerstone was the starting point of an adventure that leads to true wisdom.

With all the Freemasonic rigmarole taking place on Capitol Hill at this time, it might be asked why the particular day upon which the ceremony took place was chosen. Did it too have a specific significance within Freemasonry? It might have related to the anniversary of the signing of the American Constitution, which had taken place six years earlier in 1787. If this were the case, someone made a slight mistake because the Constitution was signed in Philadelphia on 17 September, whereas the cornerstone of the Capitol was laid on 18 September.

My research indicates that it wasn't so much the *day* that was important, either to Freemasons or to anyone else, but rather the *week* of which it was a part. The significance of this specific week of the year is now enshrined in United States law and convention, because both 17 September and 18 September are part of what is now known as Constitution Week. Constitution Week came into existence as recently as 2002, when President George W. Bush officially proclaimed 17 September to 23 September as Constitution Week.

The proclamation made by President Bush at the time suggested that the creation of Constitution Week was indeed intended to celebrate the signing of the Constitution, but if so there is something slightly odd going on. The signing of the Constitution in Philadelphia in 1787 was the final act in a prolonged meeting that had been taking place for weeks. On 18 September 1787 everyone packed their bags and went home to their various states to get the Constitution ratified, a process that took until 1790. So, for the six days after the signing of the Constitution, between 17 September and 23 September 1787, nobody was celebrating anything and the vast majority of delegates were either in the saddle or ensconced in carriages, making their way home.

So what is Constitution Week really about? Is it Freemasonic? Does it have any other significance that might have a bearing on the United States? These are questions that I thought deserved an answer. So I set out to discover what it might be.

I already had a clue because, over the last two or three decades, I have become something of an expert in historical astronomy and astrology. The period when the United States and also Washington DC came into existence is an interesting one. It was the start of a time when men of science began to gain some ground and a greater degree of credibility. This period marks a watershed between superstition and reason. Some of the founding fathers of the United States were proto-scientists – Benjamin Franklin and Thomas Jefferson, to mention two. But despite the fact that so many scientific discoveries were being made at the time, an intellectual interest in the past was also emerging. For example, there was in the 18th century a resurgence of interest in the ancient study of astrology. Astrologers studied the sky carefully because they believed that there was a direct connection between the position of the stars and planets at any given point in time and events that take place here on Earth.

The majority of scientists these days would call astrology bunkum, but that wasn't the case in 1793. The father of science, Sir Isaac Newton, had only been dead for less than five decades at the end of the 18th century. Despite his formidable reputation in science he was, first and foremost, an astrologer; a subject he studied avidly all his life. Newton wrote far more words relating to astrology than he ever did on any scientific subject, and he was certainly not alone in this fascination.

As the Age of Reason dawned, it coincided with a general resurgence of interest in the ancient world. Washington DC is itself a testimony to this because the majority of its most important and earliest structures are neoclassical in design – they deliberately reflect the artistic tastes and the architectural styles of the ancient world.

In an age when superstition was still a motivating factor, it is unlikely that any ceremony in the 18th century, especially a Freemasonic one, would be held without first consulting a learned astrologer to discover whether the stars and planets offered a positive aspect to whatever was taking place. Come to that, it is equally unlikely that the brand new United States Constitution would have been signed on a day that had not been specifically chosen for its astrological merits. The delegates in Philadelphia appear to have delayed signing the Constitution for quite a number of days, and for hitherto unknown reasons.

Anyone well versed in astrology and ancient astronomy would have no difficulty in recognizing immediately why any new venture would be likely to bode well for a long and prosperous outcome if it was celebrated at this particular part of the year. This is because the dates in question are close to the autumn equinox, one of two times each year when the Sun, which appears to rise at different points up and down the eastern horizon at dawn throughout the year, rises due east and sets due west. The other occasion is the spring equinox, which takes place in March. On the days of the spring and autumn equinoxes day and night are of equal length, and each day is taken as the start of a new season. Of the two equinoxes, the autumnal has always had the most resonance for humanity, and for a number of reasons.

Throughout the year, as seen from Earth, the Sun appears to travel through a band of space known as the ecliptic. In fact it does no such thing, and to all intents and purposes the Sun doesn't go anywhere; rather, all the planets of the solar system revolve around it. However, because we on Earth are moving at a fast rate through space, it *looks* as though the Sun is moving and that it is occupying different parts of the sky at different times of the year. The Sun seems to change its place relative to the fixed stars – a line-of-sight effect that is caused by our own movement.

In addition, the Earth's angle of inclination relative to the Sun is what gives us our seasons. In the spring and summer the northern hemisphere of the Earth is getting more sunlight and longer days. As a result it is warmer; while in the autumn and winter it is the southern hemisphere that gets the lion's share of the sunlight and day length.

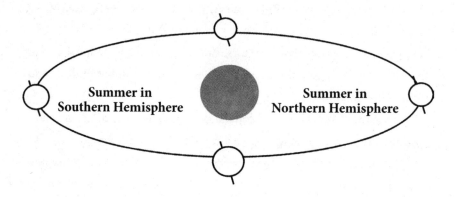

Figure 1. The angle of the Earth relative to the Sun is what allows seasons to take place upon the Earth

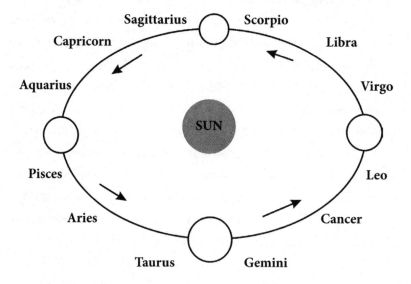

Figure 2. The background sky was split, at least in the minds of early observers, into 12 sections or signs; this is known as the zodiac

Many thousands of years ago patterns or groups of stars that lay around the ecliptic were given specific names, so that the Sun, Moon and planets could be accurately tracked at any point in time to a particular part of the sky. This was not only useful to astrologers but also to farmers and mariners. There are 12 such groups of stars (constellations) and they are collectively known as the zodiac. However, most observers didn't use the constellations; for reasons we need not go into here, they used a slightly different subdivision of the plane of the ecliptic, called the 'zodiac signs'. These had the same names as the constellations, but they subdivided the ecliptic on the basis of the Earth's seasons. That is, they were anchored into the solstices and equinoxes. The period between a solstice and the following equinox, or between that equinox and the next solstice, was divided into three zodiac signs. Astrology works by this system of subdivision of the ecliptic.

At the time of the autumn equinox, as seen from the Earth, it appears that the Sun is at the end of the zodiac sign of Virgo. The autumn has always been considered the most joyful time of year and for obvious reasons. This marks the period or culmination of harvest time in the northern hemisphere. At this part of the year the bounty of the Earth comes forth with cereal grains and fruits that can be stored for the long winter months ahead.

Virgo means 'the Virgin' and it has always been associated with the Earth Goddess. This is hardly surprising when one considers that, in pre-Christian and even pre-Judaic times, humanity worshipped a multitude of gods and goddesses, of which the Goddess of the Earth seems to have been an important and almost universal example. In the European Neolithic period this Great Goddess, as she is often known, was a predominant focus of veneration across a great deal of Europe and probably far beyond.

The Sun passes through the sign of Virgo at harvest time and it would appear that this was very important to many of our ancestors. To many cultures the Sun represented the Sky God, and so it might reasonably be suggested that at this particular time of year the Sky God had communion with the Earth Goddess, the result of which was the fruitfulness of the Earth. This is not simply conjecture because it is enshrined in belief patterns from a host of different ancient cultures.

Much of astrology works on the sort of 'sympathetic magic' of which our species was once so fond. So, for example, it stands to reason that in the mind of the unknowing observer any project or endeavour undertaken when nature was at its most bountiful would almost certainly lead to a positive and fruitful outcome. This might serve to explain why the Constitution of the United States was signed at the relevant part of September and why the cornerstone of the Capitol was also laid at this time.

However, the real focus in an astrological sense would be the actual day of the autumn equinox, which takes place around 21 September each year. In neither case was this specific day chosen. Taking these facts together with the later creation of Constitution Week, I cast around for some event or festival that might have involved the Goddess and which spanned a period up to and including the day of the autumn equinox. I did not have to look far because I was already quite familiar with one, and it came from exactly the same period and the same culture that inspired the neoclassical architecture of Washington DC.

Until around AD 400, Athens, in Greece, together with a location around 20 miles away known as Eleusis, was the scene of the most important and well-attended celebration of the Earth Goddess to take place in ancient times. This was the Mystery of Demeter, which began around 14 September and continued until after the celebration of the Mystery on 19 September in Eleusis. These dates were slightly variable because there was a lunar component to the ancient Greek calendar, which meant that, unlike our months, Greek months did not always start on the same day of the year each time. The operative time for the Demeter celebrations was the last week running up to the autumn equinox.

To the Greeks, Demeter was the goddess of vegetation – she was the predominant Earth Goddess. They believed it was Demeter that taught agriculture to humanity and, in addition to being responsible for growing things, Demeter was also closely associated with death and the afterlife. This is not too surprising because, for countless generations before the ancient Greeks carved themselves a niche in the Aegean, people had been farming and therefore monitoring the cycles of nature. They saw large parts of nature die back and disappear at the start of each winter, to be resurrected the following spring, ultimately bringing forth its bounty in terms of its fruits in the autumn. Death and rebirth were annual events and to equate them with birth, growth and death in human beings would only seem natural. This view of life was endemic to most early farming cultures.

While we do know *when* the rites of Demeter took place in Athens and Eleusis, we do not know specifically what happened to those who took part, especially during that section of the celebration known as the *Mystery*. Aspirants would gather, usually many thousands of them, in Athens around the beginning of the third week in September. Certain ceremonies took place in Athens, which included bringing ritual objects from a temple dedicated to Demeter. These would be venerated and then those taking part would walk to the sea, where they would ritually bathe and also wash piglets that were destined to become part of the ceremonies.

Only three days after the gathering had started did all the aspirants travel, in procession, to the little settlement of Eleusis. The place was held as sacred because Demeter was thought to have appeared there in person, ordering a temple dedicated to her to be built there. It was in Eleusis that the actual Mystery took place. We know very little about this, purely and simply because it *was* a mystery. Those who took part were warned on pain of death not to divulge anything that took place in the depths of the extensive building created for the purpose.

We know the ceremony involved eating barley cakes and drinking some substance that could easily have contained intoxicants. We also have sufficient contemporary evidence to be sure that it involved a death-and-rebirth enactment in which each devotee took part. New aspirants had a sponsor – someone who had been through the ceremony before – who could guide them on their own individual journey. Whatever did take place at Eleusis must have been impressive because people came from all over the known world to the celebrations and talked about its significance, often for the rest of their lives. What they never did was to explain in detail exactly what took place in the depths of the temple in Eleusis. Over a period of more than a thousand years, literally millions of people must have taken part in the Mysteries of Demeter and they were only stopped from doing so with great difficulty by a jealous Christian Church around AD 400.

Gods and goddesses in the ancient world often had a very complicated pedigree and Demeter was no different. The Greeks had their own stories to describe her but it is now accepted that she was probably already fairly ancient when her worship came to Greece. The favourite contender for the origination of Demeter is the Mediterranean island of Crete. The culture that flourished there as Europe's first super-civilization, which we know as the Minoan culture, had already gone into a rapid decline long before Athens grew to greatness. However, even some of the ancient Greeks them-selves suggested that Demeter had come from Crete and there is a wealth of Minoan evidence in the form of frescoes, pottery, statues and ritual sites to indicate that a vegetation goddess virtually identical to Demeter was number one in their pantheon of deities. This connection between Demeter and Minoan Crete will become more significant as my story unfolds.

Bearing in mind those specific dates chosen for the signing of the United States Constitution and the laying of the cornerstone of the Capitol in Washington DC, and also taking note of the creation of Constitution Week, albeit at a very recent time, could there be any connection at all between the Mysteries of Demeter and the founding of the United States, and in particular Washington DC? The reader would be right to consider any connection to be tenuous at this stage in our investigation, but there are certain factors that make it more likely, even before we start to look at the hard evidence.

Most notable is the fact that those who created Washington DC chose to adopt a style of architecture that was identical to that used in Greece at the time the Demeter celebrations were held there. To the casual observer the Capitol itself is nothing less than a Greek temple standing in an elevated position, as such temples often did. It is self-evidently a temple – in this case a temple dedicated to democracy, another legacy of Athens and Greece. It was referred to as such by those who founded it.

It has frequently been suggested, and with good evidence, that Washington DC is predominantly a Freemasonic city. We have seen just how significant Freemasons were to the cornerstone-laying ceremony for the Capitol, with even the President himself being proud to sport his Freemasonic apron during the proceedings.

There is little doubt that the assembled Freemasons on that day considered the Capitol to be extremely significant in terms of their own beliefs and practices. There were many Freemasons present at the signing of the Constitution a few years earlier and it is well known that a significant number of Freemasons were signatories of the Declaration of Independence. The number is not as high as some commentators have claimed; at least nine of the signatories were known to be Freemasons and there are suspicions about a number of others. However, it might be suggested that 9 out of 55 is still a high proportion and, in any case, those who would go on to lead the new country, for example George Washington had strong Freemasonic credentials and probably the greatest influence.

Freemasonic belief and practice cannot be divorced from the origins of a free United States and almost everyone agrees that the Craft had a strong influence on the founding of the republic, during the war that secured its freedom from Britain and at almost every stage thereafter. Freemasonry was the resort of intellectuals, men who understood about history, science, astronomy and mathematics. It also contained within its ranks many historians and, probably most important of all, it is centred on equality and fraternity. The aims and objectives of the infant United States were precisely those of the Freemasonic lodges and though many Americans these days are loath to admit or take account of Freemasonic influence in the founding of their nation, there is surely no doubt that it was a crucial factor.

So, was it the Freemasons who decided on these crucial September dates, scanning the heavens to secure the best and most propitious days for crucial ceremonies? If so, when it came to founding Washington DC, were they taking account of the ancient Mysteries of Demeter? This might not seem too likely until we lift the cover on Freemasonry to establish what actually lies at its heart. Like the Rites of Demeter, the true beliefs and even some of the practices of Freemasonry remain shrouded in mystery – so shrouded in fact that even many Freemasons have no idea what is really taking place in their midst. Freemasonry has rightfully been called 'the last mystery religion' and it might therefore not seem too surprising if it is somehow associated with earlier mystery religions. In a subsequent chapter we will take Freemasonry apart, stone by stone, and learn just how significant both the Goddess and the ancient mystery religions are to its symbolism and its very existence.

On top of the stately dome of the Capitol in Washington DC is the statue of a female figure. She wears a mixture of neoclassical clothes and those inspired by the dress of native Americans. She is called 'the Goddess of Freedom', or alternatively 'the Goddess of Armed Freedom'. This colossal bronze statue faces east. It has been suggested that this is because the main entrance to the Capitol is in the east, but the real reason is just as likely to be that she gazes towards the direction of dawn, the start of each new day. The east has always been the direction of birth and new beginnings, just as surely as the west is the direction of death and endings. It is entirely appropriate that she should be placed in what is the second highest position within the city of Washington (only the Washington Monument is higher). On the day of the autumn equinox in September, Freedom stares straight into the orb of the rising Sun as it cuts the horizon beyond Capitol Hill. At this time the Sun is stationed at the end of the zodiac sign of Virgo, a part of the sky that is also an important component of the pedigree of the Goddess of Freedom, and indeed of the Goddess by any one of a thousand names.

If the Goddess of Freedom had already been present on that Wednesday in September of 1793, at 3.30am, a full three hours before dawn, she would have seen the spectacular form of the planet Venus rising above the eastern horizon. Over in the west, the near-full moon was about to set, leaving Venus in the east for two hours as the brightest and most significant object in that early autumn morning sky. This state of affairs was not a random chance event.

To any competent astrologer it would be obvious that the day had been carefully chosen because, as surely as Virgo is the zodiac sign of the Goddess, so Venus is her planet. There would be no more propitious start to an endeavour such as the building of the Temple of Democracy, than to have Venus in such a prominent position and the Sun firmly positioned in the sign of Virgo. The day of the week was Wednesday, which from a symbolic point of view was also significant because Wednesday is the day most associated with the sign of Virgo.

We need to look more closely at the Goddess of Freedom, and to take into account the other names she possesses as far as the United States is concerned. She is part of a legacy that goes back so far into the mists of prehistory that it is quite impossible to know exactly when she was first venerated. We may think in this age of reason and science that we have no need for such superstition, and that we have left the ancient Goddess behind for good. But if this is what we thought, we would be very wrong.

CHAPTER TWO

THE GODDESS OF A THOUSAND NAMES

The Evolution of the Goddess Columbia

D espite the fact that Washington DC is such a new city, still less than 250 years old, it came at the end of an extremely ancient legacy as far as humanity on our planet is concerned. In order to establish exactly what that legacy was and the bearing it had on the infant United States we will need to embark on a series of journeys back in time. The first of these takes us many miles from the shores of America and into the remote past of Europe and Asia.

In 1997 I published a book called *The Bronze Age Computer Disc*.[3] It was about a strange little clay artefact known as the Phaistos Disc which dates back to around 2000 BC. The Phaistos Disc was found in Crete and belonged to the Minoan civilization that flourished on the island and throughout its satellite states. My interest in the Phaistos Disc lay in the patterns and hieroglyphs that cover both its surfaces. These betrayed the existence of a very particular form of calendar, also demonstrating the presence in ancient Crete of a sophisticated system of geometry and measurement long before anyone thought such a thing had been developed.

The necessary research to understand the disc involved me in an

Figure 3. Side A of the Phaistos Disc
Figure 4. Side B of the Phaistos Disc

in-depth study of the Minoan people and their lives. Despite a wealth of artefacts having come to light from the Minoan period, both in Crete itself but also as far away as the shores of the Near East, the Minoans are not half as well understood or one tenth as popular with historians and the public as their nearby neighbours in Egypt. This is not only a reflection of the tremendous age and power of Egyptian civilization, but also because it left a written legacy that has told us so much about its past. The Minoans, on the other hand, left fewer examples of their written language, and the examples we do possess have resisted all attempts to fully understand them, mainly because we don't even know what language the Minoans spoke.

The Minoans got their name in fairly recent times from the semi-legendary King Minos. The name was given to the civilization by an English archaeologist, Sir Arthur Evans. At the start of the 20th century Evans, a scholar, had read historical Greek literature extensively. He noticed that the name of Crete cropped up time and again in the oldest of the Greek myths and he kept coming across references to a powerful civilization that once existed on the island.

Eventually he was able to procure land near the north shore of Crete where a few archaeological artefacts had been turning up, and he started an extensive and long-lasting dig on the site. What he found was the famed palace of Knossos, a place that was so complicated and extensive that it un-doubtedly gave its name to the labyrinth mentioned in the famous Greek story of Theseus and the Minotaur. At Knossos, and also at many other sites throughout the island of Crete, Evans made a series of startling discoveries regarding a fabulous civilization that, apart from its place in myth, had disappeared almost entirely from history.

Part of the reason the Minoan civilization is not better known is because it was overshadowed by the later culture, that of the Mycenaeans. The Mycenaeans were the descendants of warlike tribes who had come down into the body of Greece from further north. They appeared as a cohesive culture around 1700 BC and their influence extended until around 1100 BC, which puts them firmly in the European Bronze Age. The Mycenaeans were great conquerors, which is part of the reason we know so much about them. One of their conquests, sometime between 1650 BC and 1450 BC, was Minoan Crete. This had most probably been made possible because the Minoan civilization had been all but destroyed by a catastrophic volcanic eruption on the nearby island of Santorini. Much of the artistic culture of Mycenaean Greece was a legacy of their association with Minoan Crete, which also seems to have passed at least some of its religious, cultural and artistic heritage to Greece via the Mycenaeans.

As an independent entity before the Santorini cataclysm and the Mycenaean conquest, the Minoan civilization seems to have been as close to a paradise on Earth as any culture achieved in the remote past. Crete appears to have been a very peaceful place because there are no signs that the Minoans kept a huge standing army or that the people were subjected to harsh kingship or a feudal-type hierarchy. The administration of the island seems to have been dependent upon four or five huge structures, today called palaces, in various parts of the island. Whether these were temporal or spiritual centres isn't exactly clear. There are few references to kingship in Minoan Crete but there is a great deal of iconography that tends to suggest that women played a predominant and maybe even a dominant role in Minoan society.

The Minoans were extremely artistic and were great creators of pottery in particular. They also produced massive numbers of 'seals', which were used to press symbols into wet clay in order to proclaim ownership of, say, a pythoi (jar) of wine or honey. These seal stones are still turning up all the time and many carry pictures that illuminate aspects of Minoan life.

What the richly decorated pottery, frescoes and seal stones tell us is that the Minoans were great lovers of nature and that they worshipped what seems to have been a predominant female deity, who may well have been the earlier counterpart of the later Greek Demeter. Where there is evidence elsewhere that speaks to us, the Minoans were not unique in this regard in the Mediterranean. For example, there are ancient temples in Malta, dating back as far as an incredible 4100 BC, that have huge broken statues of goddesses but no sign whatsoever of gods.

The so-called palaces of Crete, and especially that of Knossos, seem to have been as much cult centres as places of government. Within Knossos and probably the other palaces too, the Goddess seems to have been served by priestesses, many of whom are shown wearing revealing clothes and exotic hairstyles. This is in stark contrast to men, who are almost always depicted wearing nothing but a simple loincloth and who, with a few single exceptions, seem to have no ornamental dress. Men are usually shown in positions of submission, whereas the women are lively, animated and sexy.

We know that the Goddess in question was also venerated in mountain shrines and natural caves. In such settings her presence is often implied rather than explicit in any statuary. It has been suggested that simple stone pillars were her symbols, together with double-headed axes, and either she or her attendants were regularly depicted on pottery and seals.

The Minoans may not have had a great standing army – after all, for centuries they did not need one because Crete is fairly remote, and to mount a seaborne invasion before the Bronze Age would have been impossible. Nor would it be likely to have met with any success in the case of Minoan Crete because although lacking in soldiers Crete had a formidable navy. Minoan ships and sailors are mentioned extensively in Greek history and myth and it is likely that the Minoan sailors dealt with piracy in the region around their island home, as well as travelling for great distances to trade and to obtain commodities that Crete did not possess. Chief amongst these was tin – a crucial component together with copper for making bronze. Minoan Crete was a Bronze Age culture and if it wanted to get all the metal it needed its sailors almost certainly travelled even all the way to Cornwall in southwest England to procure the tin.

In return for tin and copper the Minoans could offer wool, exquisite pottery, gold jewellery and, most famous of all, honey. Vast magazines of storage vessels were found in the palaces, especially at Knossos, where commodities such as honey seem to have been gathered, either for local consumption or with transhipment in mind.

Minoan Crete was sophisticated – for example Knossos had extensive drainage, bathrooms and even a flushing toilet, as well as building techniques that were put in place to alleviate damage caused by frequent earthquakes. There is no evidence of starvation or hardship during this period and this might be partially due to the habit of stockpiling food in central locations against times of famine. Not that there is likely to have been much of a shortage for most of the time. A laughing Cretan farmer once told me the soil was so fertile that if you were to plant a stone in it, the stone would be sure to grow into something.

The Minoans were literate and had a written language that is today known as Linear A. It was used extensively at the palaces and on seals but despite exhaustive attempts it has proved impossible to decipher. A later version, known as Linear B, *is* understood, but that came into use during the Mycenaean period and relates to a language that is known. The Minoans, on the other hand, spoke in an unknown tongue, which makes it almost impossible to fathom what the Linear A characters mean.

In addition to being literate, the Minoans were also highly numerate and possessed a system of standardized weights and measures. As Chris Knight and I went on to discover, thanks to the findings of Canadian J. Walter Graham, they also understood geometry. In addition, research undertaken at Glasgow University some years ago shows that the zodiac with which we are so familiar in the West originated at a time and in a location that could only have been Crete during the zenith of Minoan power and influence; so they also clearly understood the sky – as all good sailors need to do.

Why Crete is so important in terms of the European Bronze Age is that it has left us so much from a time when hard evidence is hard to come by in other locations. It is likely that the beliefs and practices of the Minoans were not unique in their time and location. If they venerated a major female deity that later passed into the Greek pantheon as an all-powerful Earth Goddess, there is a good chance that people living around them did so too. (For example, we know this was so in Malta.)

Evidence that this was the case comes from all over Europe and parts of Asia, and from a period long before even Minoan Crete grew to greatness. Figurines depicting female forms have been found in many locations. The oldest of these, from Germany, is at least 35,000 years old. Generally known as Venus figurines, the fact that so many have been discovered surely demonstrates that they were once extremely common. Most of the Venuses

**Figure 5.
The Venus of
Willendorf; note
the enlarged
breasts, belly and
sexual organs,
whilst the face,
arms and feet have
been generally
ignored**

depict women of an ample stature, often with the sexual organs and breasts much enlarged. The Venus of Willendorf is a good example.

The bodies of the various Venuses are often lozenge shaped, with ill-defined heads and legs but extremely detailed torsos. Many look as if they are pregnant and all look extremely well fed at a time when to be so was probably not the norm. It is true that there is no proof that these figures represent a goddess of any sort but their proliferation and the fact that they have often been found within dwellings could well attest to their having a religious significance. All of these ancient Venuses point to a period well before the advent of farming – a time when hunter-gatherers occupied all of Europe.

A great argument broke out amongst historians during the 19th and 20th centuries about the significance of the Venuses, with some claiming they were little more than an expression of Stone Age pornography, whilst others maintained they were evidence of a strongly matriarchal society. This is an argument that still rages, with advocates of the matriarchal theory pointing out that, prior to the Bronze Age, life in Western Europe amongst the early farmers seems to have been peaceful, with little sign of war or subjugation from autocratic rulers. They suggest that it predominated until groups of newcomers speaking Indo-European languages gradually pushed across Europe, at which time life changed significantly. Before this insurgence, burial practices had shown no preference as to rank or gender, whereas after it warrior burials became much more common. They claim that a more warlike society is likely to be patriarchal in nature, with women adopting a subservient role.

In terms of an acceptance of a predominant female deity, this argument may well be something of a diversion. After all, Demeter was an extremely popular deity in Greece for centuries, yet the lot of women in Greece at the time was not to be envied. Women in ancient Greece were second-class citizens in every sense of the word; their primary role was to look after the home and to raise children. When it came to the running of the state, even in a local sense, they had no role to play whatsoever. If we look at a modern example we can see that in Hinduism, a religion that has at least one billion devotees in the world today, goddesses are still extremely important, but Hinduism does not advocate or demonstrate a matriarchal society.

In terms of religious belief and practice the truth is that the shunning of an acceptance that godhead is partly male and partly female is a relatively modern diversion, particularly in terms of the amount of time human beings have been active on the Earth. The single, patriarchal deity that predominates in Judaism, Islam and Christianity is not all that old. It is clear from the Old Testament of the Bible that even at the time of King Solomon, probably around 1000 BC, worship of a dominant female deity was still taking place amongst those who would eventually become the Jews. Certainly it had disappeared by the time Christianity sprang out of Judaism, but Christianity did not begin to have a real influence on the world until after the 4th or 5th centuries AD. Islam, meanwhile, which stems from the same sources, did not even come into existence until a little later.

The subjugation of the Goddess has been a very long process but part of the reason it took place was undoubtedly the advent of farming. Some notable experts have suggested that during our hunter-gatherer days the connection between sexual intercourse and the birth of a child may not have been recognized by most cultures. If this sounds absurd in light of today's knowledge we have to remember that in the case of human beings there is a full nine months between any potential sex act and the birth that results from it. Prior to the truth becoming apparent, it would have seemed as though something magical happened to women as their bellies began to swell and they eventually gave birth to new human life. Women were a reflection of the very Earth itself because they created new life. As a result they were undoubtedly revered by men as being synonymous with the Great Goddess herself. After all, apart from hunting and contributing to protection for the tribe, men appeared to contribute nothing to the creation of future generations.

With the advent of farming, people were in much closer contact with livestock and it must have eventually dawned on farmers that there was a direct connection between sexual intercourse and birth. After all, if a farmer kept a field of ewes and never introduced a ram, none of the ewes would ever bear a lamb. But if he allowed a ram to run with the ewes he would have lambs a-plenty. Once the connection was made in the human mind, things slowly began to change. Now the man could feel that the primary responsibility for new human life was his, because, similar to his ewes, if a woman never took part in sexual intercourse she would never have a child.

At the same time the farmer was now planting crops and was not relying solely on providence supplied by the Great Goddess in terms of wild grains, fruits, nuts and roots. In a sense he was *commanding* the Earth to grow what he wanted, as he could command his weaker female mate to take part in that act he now knew led to childbearing. As long as the ground received rain and the plants had sufficient sunshine, plants would grow. Sun and rain were not within the direct remit of the Earth Goddess, but were the prerogative of the 'Sky and Storm God'. It eventually became more prudent to placate him than to waste too much time on the Goddess. The Storm God could withhold his bounty, or else send so much rain that the plants would be washed away. Here comes another important connection in the mind of the early farmer: even the Earth Goddess could not send forth her bounty if the Storm God withheld the rain or sent too much of it. So it seemed that the Goddess was subservient to the God, just as woman became subservient to man.

But this was a long and convoluted process. To many societies the Goddess remained important, and even if she lost some of her significance there were aspects of life that required her protection and intervention. As a result we might say with some authority that only in the last thousand years has the world as a whole been dominated by cultures that accept the existence of a single, masculine deity, though many millions of people across the planet today still accept the relevance of a female aspect to godhead.

Even then the story is not so clear-cut. There are more than 2 billion Christians in the world today, of which well over 1 billion are Catholics and almost 250 million are Orthodox Christians. In theory, all Christians are wedded to the acceptance of one male deity, but both these sections of Christianity afford a rank and station to the Virgin Mary, mother of Jesus, that is open to scrutiny.

The Virgin Mary is not officially part of the godhead but in a way this is an intellectual abstraction. By far the majority of Catholics and Orthodox Christians consider that the Virgin Mary *is* a deity in every sense of the word except in Church law. She is prayed to across the planet on a daily basis and is the focus of intense devotion throughout several continents. To both Catholics and the Orthodox she is the 'God bearer' and enjoys the titles 'Mother of God' and 'Queen of Heaven'. This is because in Christian theology Jesus is 'as one' with God, and since Mary gave birth to Jesus, it follows that she is the 'Mother of God'. It might be suggested that in some way this means she *predates* God.

Many practising Christians would argue with this analysis but I talk about the way Christianity *is*, and not a system of fundamental doctrines that mean little or nothing to millions of ordinary worshippers. A few years ago I was undertaking research in Malta. Together with my wife I visited a large number of churches across the island and I was positively stunned by what we found. Everywhere we went there were life-sized effigies of the Virgin Mary – far more than there were representations of Jesus. Mary is positively adored in Malta. In the minds of the patrons of any one of the

365 Catholic churches across Malta it doesn't matter one jot what the Vatican says about her position within the Church. Any alien visitor to Malta who knew little or nothing about Christianity would surely be left in no doubt that the Maltese openly worship a single, powerful female deity.

Malta is far from being alone in this regard. In Latin America, which has more Catholics than any other part of the world, the same reverence for the Virgin Mary exists and, although ostensibly prayers that are sent in her direction are intended for re-routing to Jesus or to God, Mary is, to all intents and purposes, a deity in her own right.

Race memories are not easy to erase. The Christian Church may have taken the feminine out of godhead, but it could not eradicate the Goddess from people's hearts. There will be many who disagree but, to my way of thinking, the Goddess is as alive and well now for the greatest number of Christians across the planet as she was before Christianity even appeared. All that has altered is her name. As we shall see, many of her functions and characteristics have remained unchanged.

Even in Islam, with over 1.5 billion devotees in the world, a religion often cited as the most extreme example of a totally patriarchal society dedicated to an equally patriarchal godhead, there is the recognition of the female principle. In the very first sura of the Quran, in a prayer recited by Muslims across the world every day, God is known as *Al Rahmin*. Rahmin derives from a word meaning 'womb', indicating that God is not merely a masculine principle.

It seems that, just as surely as people have always needed their gods, they have always needed their goddesses too. All of life is dependent on the female principle and if the Earth with its abundance is to have any gender at all, it cannot fail to be female. Ancient people knew this and most had a multitude of goddesses to reflect the fact. Some were more popular than others. To the Greeks it was Demeter, whilst to the Egyptians the most beloved goddess of all was Isis. In Mesopotamia she was Ishtar, to the

Indo-Iranians she was Ushas and in China she was 'Queen Mother of the West'. She has been Ashtar, Lilith, Pachamama, Gaia, Terra Mater, Durga and so many other names that the list seems virtually endless because she appears in so many different forms. Rarely has a human culture existed, until the relatively modern era, that has failed to recognize the importance of a primary Earth Goddess. If the evidence offered by the multitude of Venus figurines from prehistory is to be accepted as representative of an endemic Goddess cult, then worship of life, fertility and the Earth personified in female form has been taking place for at least 40,000 years.

With such a background and pedigree, is it likely that all trace of the Goddess could be eradicated from people's hearts and minds, even across a few centuries?

As far as the United States is concerned, my research has shown that the predominant versions of the Great Goddess that were most important to its foundation, and especially to the planning and building of Washington DC, were the Greek Demeter and the Egyptian Isis. These are also the goddesses that lie at the heart of Freemasonry. It is true that in the United States the Goddess we are about to discover carried a wealth of names and was rarely referred to as either Demeter or Isis. More commonly she is either known as *Liberty* or *Columbia* but, when all the evidence is in place, I hope the reader will agree that there is little doubt who she actually represents.

There were great similarities between Demeter and Isis. Both were extremely ancient goddesses and each became associated with an enduring story that itself may be many thousands of years old. This is the story of the sacrificed and risen god. In the Demeter story the god in question is Dionysus, who himself has a close connection with the Earth and its bounty, since he had at first been a god of the corn and also gained a special responsibility for wine. In some of the Greek tales Dionysus was the child of Demeter and Zeus, king of the gods. Hera, the wife of Zeus, was jealous of the child; she turned him into a goat and he was eaten by the Titans. All that survived was his heart and this was given to Zeus. Zeus, in turn, gave the heart to Semele, a mortal woman, who consumed it and then gave birth to a reincarnated Dionysus.

Meanwhile, in Egypt, Isis was also a fertility and nature goddess. She was married to Osiris, another extremely popular god. Osiris became the object of jealousy for his brother, Set, who eventually sealed Osiris into a coffin and set it adrift on the Nile. The ever-faithful Isis eventually discovered the coffin and was able to bring it back to Egypt, where she concealed it for safety amongst reeds on the Nile. Not content, Set now tore the body of Osiris into many pieces and distributed these around Egypt. Isis recovered all the pieces and reconstructed them but the phallus was missing. Some stories say that Isis breathed life back into Osiris, and as a result became pregnant with his son, Horus. Other tales suggest that Isis constructed a phallus out of beeswax, with which she impregnated herself. In both cases Horus was considered to be a reincarnation of Osiris, who ultimately became the god of the underworld.

At their heart both these stories carry the memory of an enduring myth that seems to be extremely ancient because it is found in so many other places across the world. It is the story of the dying and reborn god of the corn. The symbolism is obvious. In the autumn the corn must be cut and humanity is dependent on the harvest for its own survival. Corn was considered to be a deity in its own right and, because it was part of the fruitfulness of the Earth, it was considered a child of the Goddess. The Goddess, synonymous with the Earth, was perpetual, and humanity was dependent on her annual resurrection of the corn.

At some stage, probably very early in our history, it occurred to people that if the Great Goddess could resurrect the corn each year, she could do the same for her devotees. It was with this precept as a backdrop that the mystery religions began to take shape. A mystery religion is a belief pattern that is responsive to certain forms of worship or actions allowed only to devotees. These are invariably kept as a secret from disbelievers and in almost all cases the mystery rituals are related to death and rebirth. This was certainly the case with regard to the mysteries of both Demeter and Isis, but there were many other examples of mystery religions in the ancient world.

At its heart, Christianity is a mystery religion, with all the hallmarks of having been so almost from the very start. Looked at from the perspective of an outsider, Jesus can be seen as yet another representative of the Corn God. Each year in church services all over the world his death and resurrection are celebrated. Like many other corn gods, Jesus was born of a virgin mother, as was the case with Isis and Horus/Osiris. If the connection between Christianity and the mysteries is doubted, we need only look at what took place on the night before Jesus was crucified, as described in the New Testament. He broke bread and passed it to his disciples, saying 'Eat, this is my body'. He took wine and gave them the cup, telling them 'Drink, this is my blood'. It is hard to see how much more specific a corn god could be.

I do not intend to belittle Christianity. I was brought up, myself, in a Christian household and I still try to live by the precepts instilled in me as a child. An acknowledgement of this particular aspect of the developing faith does nothing in my mind to detract from its significance or relevance to my life.

It is entirely likely that this section of the Christian story was added specifically so that Christianity in its early days could compete with the popular mystery religions that surrounded it. On the other hand, it isn't out of the question that Jesus deliberately played out the ritual to demonstrate that the new faith did have the required hallmarks of the mysteries. Those who partake of the sacrament 2,000 years later fully expect to be resurrected to a new life once their present life on Earth is over, and this was the same promise gained from the mysteries of Demeter and Isis. In terms of the sacrament, Christianity truly is a mystery religion. The majority of Christians believe that, at the time the bread and wine is offered during the communion, it becomes magically transformed into the *actual* body and blood of Jesus.

This belief, known as *transubstantiation*, stands at the heart of the Christian mystery and it is probably not all that different from what took place during the mysteries of Demeter and Isis, because we know that in both cases grain-based food and wine were offered to aspirants.

Just prior to the advent of Christianity much of Western Europe was under the heel of Rome, which had a huge empire extending east as far as Egypt, west as far as Britain and south into northern Africa. It included France, the Balkans, Iberia and parts of Germany. It was the Romans who adopted Christianity as the official religion of its failing empire. This happened during the reign of the Emperor Constantine around AD 300, but Christianity was not universally accepted either by Roman citizens or by many of the client areas of the Empire. It took a long time for the faith to extend to all parts of the old Roman world and pockets of paganism endured for many centuries.

Rome had always been liberal in its attitude towards religion. Roman rulers didn't generally care what anyone believed, just as long as that belief did not get in the way of the successful running of the Empire. The Romans themselves had many gods and goddesses, and they adopted many more from client peoples. One of these was Isis, whose worship became widespread throughout the Roman Empire and even in Rome itself. Other Romans would have travelled to Greece to take part in the Demeter Mysteries because, from start to finish, the Romans were fascinated by Greece and its history.

Gradually, after the adoption of Christianity by the Roman Empire, it infiltrated most areas of Europe. On the way it undoubtedly altered some of its core practices to accommodate such an eclectic mix of races. Gods and goddesses of other beliefs were absorbed into Christianity and many became the semi-legendary saints of the early Christian Church. Some of these are still revered today, for example St Bridget, originally a patron goddess of peoples living across wide areas of the north of England and probably much further afield in the Celtic world.

The Goddess of old never quite disappeared from Christianity because she was transformed into the Virgin Mary. This allowed devotees of the old Goddess to become part of the Christian Church and, although some of the practices altered, the Virgin Mary served much the same purpose in the mind of devotees as the Goddess had done. Most of the worshippers in the early Christian churches had no idea what was happening in any case. Services were conducted entirely in Latin. Bibles were also in Latin and even this was of little consequence because very few people could read.

Anyone from a family that simply refused to accept Christianity, preferring to stick to the old ways, was eventually faced with prosecution by the Church and possible execution. As I explained in *The Goddess, the Grail and the Lodge*,[4] there is ample evidence that such families did exist and continued to do so for many centuries. They stayed safe by *appearing* to pay lip service to Christianity, while actually doing their own thing. I am not alone in suggesting that this was the case. Most commentators have merely hinted at the possibility, but some were willing to allow their knowledge on the subject to be known, even if it was through words of fiction. The well known and much loved British Victorian novelist, Anthony Trollope, clearly had a good idea of what could take place under the cover of the Church. Trollope was a Freemason and he might well have been actually talking about himself when he described a character from one of his books, *Barchester Towers*. The individual in question is called Mr Thorne, who was also a Freemason, and this is what Trollope has to say about Thorne when describing his religious attitude and behaviour:

… He, however, and others around him, who still maintained
the same staunch principles of protection – men like
himself, who were too true to flinch at the cry of a mob
– had their own way of consoling themselves. They were,
and felt themselves to be, the only true depositories left of
certain Eleusinian Mysteries, of certain deep and wondrous
services of worship by which alone the gods could be rightly
approached. To them and them only was it now given to
know these things, and to perpetuate them, if that might still
be done, by the careful and secret education of their children.

We have read how private and peculiar forms of worship
have been carried on from age to age in families, which to
the outer world have apparently adhered to the services of
some ordinary church. And so it was by degrees with Mr
Thorne … Nor was he without a certain pleasure that such
knowledge, though given to him, should be debarred from
the multitude.[5]

The passage speaks for itself, and it specifically mentions the word
'Eleusinian', which of course relates to Eleusis, the place close to Athens
where the Mysteries of Demeter were held annually. Trollope, who had a
second-to-none understanding of the Church of his day, knew quite well
that there were people within the Church whose real views were radically
different to those of the institution to which they appeared to belong. He
may have been one of them himself.

It is my belief that a fair proportion of people such as the fictional Mr
Thorne ultimately found their way to America, where they could practise
their own exclusive faith with impunity and where, eventually, they could
help to create a new nation in which traditional Christianity would play
little or no part. These men were not necessarily anxious to force their

opinions onto others – in fact, like Mr Thorne, they remained quite happy that what they knew was *not* known by 'the multitude'.

Amongst their Eleusinian beliefs was an ancient and enduring reverence for a female deity. By the late 18th century, with neoclassicism reaching fever-pitch and with all things ancient being revered by society at its highest levels, they were at last in a position to cement their personal beliefs in ways that had not been possible since Christianity had tried so hard to destroy the older mystery religions. One of the weapons these people used was Freemasonry, which might well have been created for the purpose. So before we begin to look closely at what actually took place on the border of Virginia and Maryland when Washington DC was first planned, we need to turn our attention to an institution that is still little understood, even by those within it. We need to expose Freemasonry and to learn what it is actually about.

CHAPTER THREE

A MAN'S THING

The Freemasonic Way of Thinking

No explanation of the history of Washington DC would be complete without at least a reasonably good understanding of Freemasonry. At the very start of the book I made reference to the most important ceremony that took place when the city was started, namely, the placing of the cornerstone of the Capitol. Freemasonic iconography is to be found all across Washington DC, which is not surprising since membership of the Craft was extremely common in the post-colonial United States, many leaders of which were also practising Freemasons.

When my friend and colleague Christopher Knight wrote his first book, together with Robert Lomas in 1996, he had already spent several years on the research. The book was called *The Hiram Key*,[6] and it was an attempt to explain exactly what Freemasonry is.

On the surface Freemasonry is a men's club – though of course there are now women's lodges, so even the male exclusivity isn't strictly true these days. Most men who are Freemasons go to Lodge meetings because it presents a chance to meet like-minded individuals, to socialize, have a good meal and maybe a couple of drinks. They will also be involved in raising money for various charities, many of which have nothing to do with Freemasonry itself. On the way they might get interested in what the organization is really all about – that is, if they spend enough time looking into it.

Freemasonry is not, on the surface at least, a secret society, even though there are plenty of people in the world who publish books and articles that assume from the start that this is the case. On the contrary, there is probably nothing apparent within the practices, symbols, words or role-play involved in Freemasonic meetings that is not readily accessible for anyone to see on the internet or in freely available books. Freemasons these days are making a real effort to squash the idea that their organization is either inherently secretive or exclusive. Admission to a Masonic lodge has always been open to any man of good conduct, no matter what his rank, religion or status. The only perquisite is that he is willing to confirm that he believes in a Creator of some sort.

It is true that, during the three separate ceremonies that take an aspirant from 'Entered Apprentice' through the rank of 'Fellow Craft' and onto that of a 'Master Mason', the would-be Mason has to make certain commitments and, in a piece of wordy rhetoric, he must promise not to reveal any of the secrets of the Craft. He is warned that if he does so he could be brought to task and despatched in a particularly gruesome and horrible way. None take these threats seriously these days and probably have not done so for centuries.

Freemasonry is a fraternal organization that relies heavily on symbolism. Its rituals and practices seem desperately archaic because many of them are genuinely old. Advancing through the three degrees of the Craft, until eventually reaching the rank of Master Mason, any candidate will have to learn a great many passages of dialogue by heart and take part in a series of ceremonies that might or might not be interesting but which are quite definitely obscure.

Where and when the whole business began, it is quite frankly almost impossible to know. Grand Lodge in London, which is responsible for

Freemasonry across Britain and in many cases far beyond, is adamant that Freemasonry began in the 18th century. This is self-evidently not true because it is known that Freemasonic meetings were being held in Scotland in particular, long before any took place in London.

If the language and stories of Freemasonry are to be believed it has been going on for considerably longer than the 18th century – right back to the building of King Solomon's Temple around 1000 BC. But this is where things begin to get slightly complicated because there are two distinctly different classifications of Freemasonry. According to modern Freemasonic explanations the original lodges of Freemasons were *operative*, which means the people attending the meetings actually were stonemasons, which would have made the lodges a sort of early trade union or federation.

Only in the 17th or 18th century did non-stonemasons begin to become involved in the Craft. It is likely that this began in Scotland. The story is explained in full in a book I wrote with John Ritchie called *Rosslyn Revealed*.[7] In all probability the Craft came into existence as a result of the building of a strange little supposedly-Christian chapel at Rosslyn near Edinburgh. The building is filled with all manner of esoteric secrets and its builder, William Sinclair, did not wish anyone outside of his own circle to know what the structure was really all about. In order to keep his stonemasons quiet he involved them in his secret club. It proved to be popular and eventually attracted men from the district who had nothing to do with stonemasonry. Eventually the Craft turned from being 'operative' to *speculative*. (The significance of Rosslyn Chapel was not lost on the earliest Freemasons in and around Washington DC because there is still a section of Washington DC, immediately across the Potomac from the central city, that is known to this day as Rosslyn.)

After a while, Freemasonry spread to other places and found its way into England. It was quite popular but, in a fairly heated political and religious climate, it began to look as though Freemasonry was a haven for those plotting against royalty. As a result it was completely reformed in England when the Grand Lodge was formed in 1717. The structure and much of the supposed history of the organization was changed to better suit the Protestant sensibilities of the period. People in England were paranoid at the thought of Catholicism gaining the upper hand again, after a couple of centuries of bloodshed and intrigue as Church affiliation flipped back and forth between Rome and Canterbury. Some of the Scottish Freemasons especially had Jacobite, and therefore Catholic, credentials and this could simply not be tolerated in England.

As a result, if we want to see what Freemasonry was originally about we have to look as far back in time as we can, which isn't easy since many of the earliest Scottish lodges did not keep very good records, either of membership or procedures. Very little was written down in early Freemasonry. Rather it was passed on by word of mouth and learned by rote – a necessary prerequisite at a time when even a great many fairly well-to-do people were still semi-literate or illiterate.

All Freemasons have to pass through the obligatory three degrees to reach the highest rank of Master Mason. Beyond that they can become officers of a lodge and, in some forms of Freemasonry, they can also go on to achieve other degrees, each one related to a different historical subject and each intended to add to the moral fibre of the Mason in question. Some of these advanced degrees are religious and Christian in nature, but this was never the original intention of the Craft, which from the start has been open to men of all religious persuasions.

Achieving the three necessary degrees requires a certain amount of role-play, a number of different costumes and the participation of other lodge members. But as Chris Knight discovered, most of what was said and done appeared to be nonsense, which is why he set out to investigate whether there was anything underpinning Freemasonry that was either deliberately covered up or which had been forgotten over the years.

Originally, and especially in places like London, lodges (just another name for a particular group of Freemasons) were often tied to a trade or a profession. There were lodges for printers, solicitors, bankers, judges, the police and all manner of other groups. (As a good example, there were specific lodges for soldiers on both sides in the American War of Independence.) As a result, people started to reason that Freemasonry was little more than a self-help group, in which individuals could gain financially from mixing with the right people. Undoubtedly there has been some truth in this, and it may still be, even now, that lodges tend to be more eclectic. It stands to reason that if, through business, a Mason can do a favour for one of his brother Masons, he will try to be accommodating. However, this is no different for a group of people involved in an archery club, a flower-arranging circle, or even the Women's Institute. There may have been a degree of impropriety associated with Masonic lodges but probably no more than would be the case with any group or organization of like-minded individuals.

What seems to have really angered people over the years is that they simply don't know what goes on at Masonic meetings, but in this they are not in the minority because very few Freemasons are much better informed. What matters in Freemasonry to most of its members is the fellowship, the chance to talk to like-minded people from all sorts of backgrounds and the social opportunities the lodge presents. Very few Freemasons want to delve into the supposedly dark past of the organization or would know where to start doing so. If Freemasonry looks at all sinister, it does so only from the outside. Although not a Freemason myself, I have been invited to literally dozens of lodges to speak and have found nothing untoward to report.

Freemasonry has a fascination for a whole series of different historical stories, many of which are patently closer to myth than genuine history. Chief amongst these is the story that relates to the building of King Solomon's Temple in Jerusalem. According to the Masonic tale the architect of the building was a man called Hiram Abif. He alone held all the secrets of the building's construction and as a result he was an object of envy and jealousy to some of his workers. Eventually he was accosted by a group of malcontents, all demanding to know these secrets. Hiram refused to divulge them and was eventually killed because of his silence. His body was secretly buried and the guilty workers fled.

King Solomon was told about the disappearance of Hiram Abif and sent soldiers to look for him. His grave was eventually discovered; he was disinterred, given a decent burial, and the guilty workers were found and executed.

At first sight this story is obviously a myth and not even a particularly convincing one. But it stands at the very heart of Freemasonry, and much of the ceremony associated with the three degrees of the Craft is tied to it. The interesting thing about this tale, and many other aspects of Freemasonry, is that it can be looked at in a number of different ways. The explanation for stories, symbols and allegory that is handed out by rote at Freemasonic gatherings and in many Freemasonic books is at best ambiguous. To those in the know it can sometimes seem downright misleading. Whether even many high-ranking Freemasons are aware of the obfuscation that is taking place seems to be in some doubt. I have given lectures to some illustrious Freemasons, especially in Scotland, and I have watched with interest the glazed eyes of my audience when I have been explaining something about which there can really be no doubt. My audience is often impressed with my explanations and I have lost count how many times some provincial Grand Master or other high-ranking Freemason has said to me: 'Do you know Alan, I've never looked at things that way.'

The truth is that these often-elderly men are passing on the explanations *they* were given for a whole host of stories and symbols. Naturally, they accepted what they were told and probably had no reason to doubt it.

One potent indication that there is more to Freemasonry than meets the eye comes with the Third Degree ceremony, in which the candidate, who ritually takes the place of Hiram Abif, is symbolically killed and then ultimately raised from the dead. The general explanation for this ritual is that the Mason is dying from his former life and being reborn into the rights, privileges and responsibilities of a Master Mason. However, there are such great similarities between this ceremony and what we know took place in the Mystery Rites of Demeter, Isis and other religions of ancient times that one is forced to ask whether or not there is more to the Third Degree raising than immediately meets the eye.

Since it first occurred to me that Freemasonry might be a carefully disguised version of a much older mystery rite, I have come across a number of individuals who have independently arrived at the same conclusion. One of these was a man named Meredith Sanderson. I haven't met the man, nor indeed could I ever do so because he wrote his books on Freemasonry in the 1920s. Sanderson was a major in the army, as well as being a doctor, and he spent many years working in Africa. By today's standards his work would be considered to be on the edge in terms of its political correctness, but it is amazing to see just how close to the mark he seems to be on many points. His words in *An Examination of Masonic Ritual*[8] are intended for the eyes of fellow Freemasons and, although they are now out of print, they are freely available on the internet.

Meredith Sanderson looked deeply into Freemasonic symbolism and practice, and he did so in light of a very good working knowledge of the ways of people he called 'primitive'. He lived for many years among the tribes of central Africa and was able to gain a good understanding of many of their rites and rituals, especially those pertaining to food and sex. Sanderson was of the opinion that it is difficult, if not absolutely impossible, to differentiate between the two, since in his opinion 'primitive' people clearly lumped together the fertility of nature, which gave them food, and the fertility of individuals, which perpetuated the tribe and the species.

Sanderson's ultimate conclusion about Freemasonic practices, and in particular the raising of the aspirant to the three successive degrees, is that it harks back to a combination of 'food rites' and 'transition rites'. The latter relates to the time when a boy is taken away from his family and his tribe, undergoing a series of tests, lessons and ordeals in order to achieve manhood. Sanderson points out that by the time the boy returns to his family, maybe several weeks or months later, he has, in their eyes at least, been almost literally resurrected. He is now a man, has a different name and is party to a host of secrets that are kept from both children and women of the culture. I think there is an important point here, and it is one we will come back to later. It strikes me that with such initiation rites, no matter what culture they apply to, it is never the intention of boys who come to manhood as a result of these secret rites to pass their newfound knowledge to anyone at all who is not part of their 'club'. Such an individual may hold his new knowledge for the good of all the people, but this knowledge is not open to any but the initiate.

Outside of the initiation or transition rites, Sanderson points to food rites. Within these there are pronounced sexual elements because, as we have seen, in what Sanderson calls 'primitive' cultures, there isn't too much differentiation between the fruitfulness of the Earth and the fruitfulness of people. He points to humanity's reliance on sympathetic magic and infers, as I have always thought, that early religion and magic observed the returning cycles of death and rebirth in nature and equated them with death and birth in human beings. In other words, if everything in nature is reborn in due season, why should not human beings also be resurrected?

A tribe with which Sanderson had a specific connection was that of the WaYao of central Africa. He explains how he had been invited to some of the sex rites of the tribe, performed only by men, and he talks of a 'pantomime' that involved the creation of effigies, which Sanderson explains would be seen in the West as grossly obscene. He goes on to suggest that the tribesmen themselves would be astounded at such an accusation, though it is clear from his slightly guarded description that pregnant women, ritual vaginas and phalluses were all part of the ceremonies he observed.

What is most interesting about Meredith Sanderson's commentary is that he is certain that the three degrees of Freemasonry have their ultimate origin in a combination of 'transition rites', and 'food rites with their sexual content', but he either fails to recognize, or else does not choose to comment that the sexual symbolism of the WaYao warriors is still present in Freemasonic symbolism at every level. True, lodge meetings do not have life-sized statues of pregnant women, or huge phalluses, but they are still there if one knows where to look.

There are some symbols that have always had sexual overtones to a wealth of different cultures for a very long time. Chief amongst these are the chevron and the diamond shape.

In the case of the chevron the symbolism is easy to see. The chevron is the same shape as the 'V' formed by a woman's pubic hair. Meanwhile the

 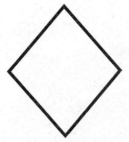 

Figure 6. The chevron; throughout history this symbol has been used to signify female sexuality because it is the same shape as a female's pubic hair

Figure 7. The diamond shape has often been associated with the female vagina

Figure 8. The *vesica pisces*; sometimes a secret representation of the human female vagina

diamond, which has also had strong sexual overtones, is not only a chevron and its mirror image, it also represents the vagina itself. A variation on the diamond is the symbol known as the *vesica pisces*, another sexual symbol from history that has been used by all manner of cultures.

Our ancestors, even our Christian ones, were not as sensitive about sexual symbolism as we tend to be these days. A good example is Figure 9, a photograph of a stone carving from a Christian church in Kilpeck, Herefordshire, England.

In this carving the female is pulling on either side of her vagina with her hands, creating within the vagina the classical vesica pisces shape. However, when seen from below it can be observed that both the chevron and the diamond are incorporated into the lower and therefore the sexual part of this carving.

Figure 9. The 12th-century stone carving known as a Sheela na Gig to be found outside the parish church of Kilpeck, Herefordshire

Nobody could deny the sexually explicit nature of such a carving and there are many other examples to be found in Britain and Ireland. There is nothing sordid or vulgar about such carvings, which represent our own versions of the effigies Meredith Sanderson observed amongst the WaYao tribesmen of central Africa. In the distant past the sexuality of our species was not hidden but rather extolled, as it still is today by less inhibited cultures than our own.

By the time Freemasonry came into vogue in the 18th century, society had become slightly more genteel. The gentlemen who frequented the Freemasonic lodges of London, or elsewhere in Britain, would not have flaunted effigies such as Sheela na Gigs during their lodge meetings, but the symbolism representing them was definitely present (*see* page 44).

When Freemasonry advertises itself in almost any situation the square and compasses is the symbol that is used, either with or without the 'G' in the centre. Both the square and the compasses are tools used in stone-masonry and, as such, they have a meaning to speculative Freemasons. To Freemasons the square is emblematic of one's relationship with others at a material level, whilst the compasses relate to a constant pursuit of spiritual knowledge and awareness. The reasoning is that any structure created using these tools will turn out to be both beautiful and functional. But is this all that is represented by this symbol? It doesn't take much imagination to see that the square and compasses arranged in this fashion creates both the chevron and the diamond.

So what of the 'G' in the centre? It isn't always present. Most Freemasons would say it represents God because that is what they have been told. But it won't come as much of a shock to most readers to realize that while God is spelt with a 'G', so is Goddess. So, let's look at the symbol again. Might it not simply be a disguised version of a Sheela na Gig figure, or something similar? All the necessary components are present. This is so typical of the symbolism of Freemasonry – it appears to say one thing but, when one is in possession of the correct information, it tells us something completely different.

It has been suggested that the square and compasses also represent a slightly disguised version of a hexagram.

Both the hexagram and the pentagram are used in Freemasonic symbolism and a hexagram can be formed by putting two horizontal lines across the points of the compass and the square. What is particularly fascinating about the hexagram is that it has six points, six sides and six small triangles within it. William Bond, author of *Goddess Symbolism within Freemasonry*[9] points out that 666 was considered a sacred number and one often associated with the Goddess, since it was representative of the Goddess in her triple form, as the virgin, the pregnant woman and the crone. The number 666 is still held as sacred in Hinduism, though to the Christian Church it is said to be the number of the Devil. This is because the number is mentioned in the Book of Revelation of the Bible. In this most fantastical of biblical books the writer equates the number 666 with what he calls 'The Whore of Babylon' – the Great Goddess. The Book of

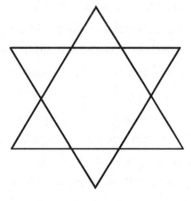

Figure 10. The square and compasses; the most enduring symbol of Freemasonry

Figure 11. A hexagram, otherwise known as the Star of David

Revelation was written in the early days of the Christian Church at a time when it was by no means certain that the faith would gain predominance over other popular beliefs. As a result we find the early Church making a devil out of someone else's most sacred deity.

Going back to the triangle and the chevron, which are both components of the hexagram, these do not appear by chance in the context of the square and compasses. They are used elsewhere by Freemasons and, in particular, they are utilized in conjunction with food. The traditional arrangement of cutlery for each place setting at a Masonic banquet is as shown in Figure 12. I am indebted to author William Bond for bringing this to my attention.

Once again the 'G' is often shown in the centre. Eating and drinking forms an important part of Masonic gatherings – as I know only too well to the cost of my waistline. The consumption of food and drink may no longer form part of the rituals in Freemasonry, as it did in the ancient Mysteries of Demeter and Isis or as it still does in the Christian Communion but, nevertheless, it represents a significant feature of most Masonic evenings. With the chevron and the diamond present on the table before him, and

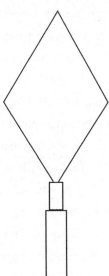

Figure 12. Cutlery setting for a Masonic banquet

Figure 13. The Masonic trowel

in the knowledge of the 'G' that rightfully belongs at their centre, the truly *knowing* Mason would recognize the presence of the Goddess at the meal. Perhaps he should, because many of our ancient ancestors would have been deeply indebted to her that they were eating at all.

Other symbols within Freemasonry are just as informative. The trowel, which is also central to the symbols and role-play, is said to represent the spreading of the cement of brotherly love (*see* page 45).

Once again we have the diamond present, together with the inferred chevron and this time also including the phallic representation of the handle.

Both Sanderson and Bond also point to the phallic nature of the two famous pillars of Freemasonry. These are representations of the two pillars that stood at the entrance to King Solomon's Temple and which are mentioned in the Old Testament. To Freemasons these pillars are called Boaz and Jachin and they are an essential component of any Masonic temple.

It is true that the pillars in question have a phallic symbolism but things might go slightly deeper than this. Previously, I made reference to the fact that, once upon a time, and across a significant geographical area, the Goddess was worshipped in the form of a pillar. We know this was the case for the pre-Judaic Semitic people, even down to the reign of King Solomon. To these people the Goddess was called Ashera. There are references to wooden pillars in sacred groves that represented her presence. The same is probably also true in Minoan Crete. Whilst there is no absolute proof in this case, it is interesting to note that in places of Goddess veneration in Minoan Crete, there is never any statue depicting the Goddess, but there are almost always pillars. Since Crete is so close to the Levant and also since it is known that the Cretans had settlements in Gaza and further inland, an association between cultures that intermixed so readily is not at all unlikely.

Alongside this we might look at the popularity in Stone Age and Bronze Age times of large standing stones. These are to be found across the islands of the Mediterranean, in Spain, France, Ireland and the British Isles. Many commentators have speculated that the tall standing stones could once have been worshipped as the deity, male or female (or possibly both).

Another important symbol in Freemasonry is the 'All-Seeing Eye' (*see* page 48). This is to be seen in a great deal of Masonic art and is obviously of the utmost importance. It has been suggested by Freemasons that the All-Seeing Eye can alternatively be known as the 'Eye of Horus'.

If, as many Freemasons believe, the All-Seeing Eye does derive from the Eye of Horus, it has an interesting pedigree. For starters it is, once again, an allegorical representation because the vagina has often been called, in slang terms, 'the eye', so this may be another representation of the vagina of the Goddess, from which everything in the world ultimately comes forth.

However, there is another connection. Although the Eye of Horus is associated with the male god Horus, its origins predate him and relate to a goddess by the name of Wadjet, one of the very earliest of the Egyptian deities. Although in later dynasties Wadjet was associated with protection for the king and royal power generally, in earlier times she appears to have been a typical representative of the sort of Great Goddess that seems to have predominated across much of Europe, Asia and Africa. In particular, she is virtually synonymous with another, later goddess named Mut. Mut was also a typical mother goddess, who was said to have presided over the primal waters that predated all of life. She was, in effect, the Goddess from whose womb everything living ultimately emerged.

The connection with the Eye of Horus comes from the fact that in Ancient Egyptian the Eye of Horus was called 'The Wadjett'. In later dynasties the right eye of Horus, who was usually depicted as a falcon, had a special significance to the Sun god, Ra, but the fact that the eye itself

Figure 14. The Eye of Horus, sometimes referred to as the 'All-Seeing Eye'

Figure 15. The more common form of 'All-Seeing Eye' as used in Freemasonry

retained such an early connection to a creator goddess demonstrates where it originally came from.

The All-Seeing Eye is a good example of Freemasonry following the United States, as opposed to the United States being absolutely responsive to Freemasonry. The All-Seeing Eye appears on the American dollar bill atop a truncated pyramid. It has been suggested that this shows that the United States was, or is, heavily influenced by Freemasonry. In reality the All-Seeing Eye was first suggested as part of the design for the Great Seal of the United States but it was dropped from that design and later reappeared on currency. The symbol was unknown in Freemasonry at the time the Great Seal was planned, and it did not appear in any Freemasonic context until a book called *Freemason's Monitor* by Thomas Smith Webb appeared in 1797. By that time the discussions regarding the design of the Great Seal had been over for 14 years.

Back in 1923 Meredith Sanderson was already referring to the relevance of the Corn God myths to Freemasonry, and of course these myths are directly responsive to the acceptance of a perpetual Goddess. Each year, as the corn was cut and the grain was used to sustain life for the farmers and their families, ceremonies were held to ensure that, when the seed corn was planted, it would grow strong and offer next year's harvest.

The mythical character Hiram Abif is a representative of this tradition. He and the third-degree Freemasons who take on his persona are acting out the part of the Corn God. This is why Hiram Abif is referred to in Freemasonry as 'the son of the widow'. In most of the original Corn God myths the husband and the son of the Goddess are one and the same person. It is the Corn God that couples with the Goddess to make nature bountiful, but every harvest time he is killed and the Goddess becomes a widow again. The seed corn and the sprouting plants represent her son, who in turn will grow to become her consort.

Later on, when we come to look at how astronomy had a strong influence on the infant United States, we will come across other examples of how influences associated with the founding of a nation also had a bearing on developing Freemasonry. Although it is filled with apparently archaic stories and traditions, like any other institution Freemasonry has changed significantly over the decades. In no place has that been more apparent than in the growing and developing United States, which has influenced Freemasonry every bit as much as Freemasonry has contributed to the birth and development of the United States and of course to the planning and creation of Washington DC.

CHAPTER FOUR

A NATION IS BORN

The Free United States and its Capital

S ince Washington DC was specifically built to be the capital city of the new free United States of America, it stands to reason that it came into existence directly as a result of the aspirations and desires of the new nation's citizens. It represented a tangible expression of those ideologies and in particular a desire for freedom from oppression and the right to self-determination.

The relationship between Britain and its colonies on the eastern seaboard of North America was often difficult. This isn't too surprising, and for a number of different reasons. Firstly, it was a matter of distance; it took weeks for ships to sail across the Atlantic from Britain to America. As a result, communication between the two locations was extremely slow. Decisions made in London regarding the colonies were subject to inevitable delays, not only in terms of the time it took for messages to get back and forth, but also because the king and parliament usually had to be involved. The slow pace of bureaucracy did not suit the impetuous nature of people who were genuine pioneers; nor did they feel that their wishes or opinions were being taken into account in far-off London.

It should also be remembered that many of those living in the American colonies had come there specifically to get away from certain aspects of

Britain and its institutions, with which they did not agree. The constant religious intrigues and battles that had taken place in Britain since the reign of King Henry VIII (1491–1547) had marginalized all manner of people. Henry had broken with Rome, partly because the Pope would not allow him to have the divorce he wanted, but also because a wave of Protestantism was starting to roll across Western Europe and the power of the Pope and the Catholic Church was being questioned.

It was during the reign of Henry's daughter, Elizabeth I (1533–1603) that emigration to the New World really began. Elizabeth was a Protestant and, though personally tolerant of both Catholics and other sects of Christianity, her regime hardened as plots were hatched that threatened her Crown and her life. During both Elizabeth's reign and her successors', those who felt themselves to be religiously or politically marginalized decided to seek a new life in the virgin lands beyond the great ocean.

It was not just the fracture between the Catholics and Protestants that caused problems. Once a Protestant Church was established in Britain, it too began to grow intolerant of those who felt they could not toe the Church of England line. Puritans in particular found it difficult to practise their religious devotions without being harassed by the Church of England and, together with all manner of denominations of Protestants from parts of continental Europe, they began to seek a new life far away.

Soon the British colonies in North America were beginning to prosper, but their growth and development were constantly being hampered by rules laid down in London. The British fought extensive wars with the French on American soil. These were fearfully expensive and the British government, in an attempt to recoup the massive amounts that it was spending on the army and navy, imposed ever-higher taxes on the American colonists. Britain also insisted that many commodities the colonists needed *must* be purchased from Britain, often at a higher price than they could be obtained from other sources. Discontentment festered, and it did so in an environment in which the poor and disenfranchised people of other nations, especially France, were themselves on the verge of revolution.

A whole series of events led to the inevitable confrontation that took place between Britain and its American colonies. Much of the organization of what eventually would become armed revolution took place behind the doors of Freemasonic lodges, especially in Boston but also in Philadelphia. Often, when looking at situations such as the famous Boston Tea Party, it is not possible to prove that insurrection was planned at Masonic gatherings, but there is little doubt that the cohesive structure of Freemasonry proved to be a boon when it came to getting people onside and working together.

In 1774 the first Continental Congress was convened by the discontented colonists in 13 American colonies. They petitioned the King, George III, to allow them representation in the British parliament, declaring a boycott of certain British goods, at the same time refusing to pay taxes with which they did not agree. When their pleas were ignored the Americans convened a second Continental Congress in 1775, at which they authorized the formation of a Continental Army. Britain saw this as an open threat and responded by declaring those organizing the Congress traitors, and by stating that the 13 colonies in question were in a state of rebellion. The Americans felt they no longer had any choice and, in 1776, they declared themselves to be a new nation. They rejected any further allegiance to the British King and, from that point on, considered the United States of America to be a sovereign state in its own right.

War now became inevitable. The American colonies were able to call on a great deal of assistance from France, which, although still a monarchy at the time, had its own argument with Britain, especially over areas of North America. Together with their French allies the Americans fought a clever and brave war against the British, who could never bring sufficient strength to bear in America, partly because Britain had so many military commitments elsewhere. Finally, the colonists triumphed and in 1781 the

British on the American continent surrendered and the free United States of America became a hard and fast reality.

It was soon decided that a new nation needed a capital city. There were many suggestions and Philadelphia was a prime candidate but, wherever the capital was located, if it was placed in a pre-existent city it would have caused problems. Although the 13 states had come together to fight a war, their individual views of what the United States should be differed greatly, in the main fuelled by their own individual needs. It was quite clear to George Washington and the other men leading the new nation that a federal capital could not exist within any of the original states and certainly not in an existing state capital, for fear of every other state complaining. The nation's capital could well have been Philadelphia, were it not for demonstrations that took place there in 1783; it was besieged by men who had fought for America in the War of Independence and who demanded payment. It became impossible for those governing the United States to remain in Philadelphia and they moved their base to New Jersey. Clearly there was a problem and so an addition to the Constitution was created. It gave the government the right:

> To exercise exclusive legislation in all cases whatsoever, over
> such district (not exceeding ten miles square) as may, by
> cession of particular states, and the acceptance of Congress,
> become the seat of the government of the United States, and
> to exercise like authority over all places purchased by the
> consent of the legislature of the state in which the same shall
> be, for the erection of forts, magazines, arsenals, dockyards,
> and other needful buildings.

In effect, the nation's capital would have to exist in a political no-man's-land. This would mean creating what was, to all intents and purposes, a new state that owed nothing to any of the 13. The new American government sanctioned their first free president, George Washington, to find such a location. (American Constitution, Article One, Section Eight.)

George Washington's home was in Virginia, near Alexandria, at a place called Mount Vernon. Since Washington had been charged with finding a site for the new capital it isn't especially surprising that he hit upon a location not too far from his own home. However, as we shall see, it was more than opportune. He knew the district well and in all probability the idea for a capital city in this particular location had been in his mind all along. In accord with the wishes of Congress, Washington located the new capital astride the Potomac River, encompassing a location that at the time was known as Troy. The new 'district' as it would eventually be called, would be split between the states of Maryland, considered a northern state, and Virginia, which thought of itself as a southern state. This decision pleased most people, though since the new district would also encompass Alexandria, and because Washington lived close to Alexandria in Virginia, it was decided that any legislative buildings would have to be north of the Potomac, in Maryland.

The land was purchased and George Washington formed a committee to oversee the founding of the district. He graciously accepted the suggestion that the capital city should be named Washington, after himself, but there is no hard and fast evidence as to why the name of the overall district should be 'Columbia'. I hope that in time this will become obvious.

The commissioners for the new city, all appointed by Washington, were Thomas Johnson, Daniel Carrol and David Stuart. In turn the commissioners employed Major Andrew Ellicot, with his brothers Benjamin and Joseph, together with Isaac Briggs, George Fenwick and Benjamin Banneker, to survey the site and lay down markers for the new district. They created a diamond-shaped area; in reality a square standing on its point. Each side of the diamond was to be 10 miles long (actually it wasn't, but we will deal with that presently), so that the area of the District of Columbia would be 100 square miles. Many of the stone pillars that marked the boundary of Columbia are still present. It is interesting to note that when the marker stone at Jones Point was dedicated, in April 1791, the ceremony was attended by assembled Freemasons. A newspaper account of the proceedings clearly says: '... *The Master of the Lodge and Dr Stewart, assisted by others of their brethren, placed the Stone; after which a deposit of corn, wine and oil was made upon it.*' If something sounds familiar about this, it should, because corn and wine are two of the most potent symbols of the Mysteries, whilst oil has always been used for anointing – the queen of the new district?

Once the site for the district had been fixed it became necessary to design the new city. Responsibility for this was eventually given to a French architect and engineer by the name of Pierre Charles L'Enfant. L'Enfant had fought for the Americans in the War of Independence under the famous Major General Lafayette. He was injured in battle but recovered and eventually became part of General Washington's personal staff.

L'Enfant set to work with a passion. History relates that he planned the city initially based upon a right-angled triangle. One corner of this would be located on a hill that L'Enfant declared to be a 'pediment waiting for a monument'. Here he intended the new American seat of government to be placed.

The base of the triangle would travel west from this point and, at the point where it turned north, L'Enfant intended a statue commemorating George Washington to be placed. The upright of the triangle would lead north to the president's house (now the White House) and a grand road, now Pennsylvania Avenue, would mark the hypotenuse as it travelled southeast to complete the triangle at the Capitol building.

Everything else in the city would be laid out in and around this triangle and L'Enfant intended it to be the grandest city in the world, with a grid street plan, many grand intersections and lots of parks. Diagonal avenues would cross the gridiron streets, which would be built north–south, and at the intersections there would be circles with statues and gardens. The president's house in particular would be huge – over five times the size it turned out to be.

Everything went well at first but it turned out that L'Enfant was not the easiest person in the world to deal with. Although he created an initial plan, he was late providing a finished engraving of his intended city, mainly because his plans constantly changed. L'Enfant was supposed to co-operate with Thomas Jefferson and the three appointed commissioners, but arguments ensued. Eventually, mainly because L'Enfant refused to concentrate the limited resources on the federal buildings, he was sacked.

L'Enfant's plan was somewhat modified by Andrew Ellicot and this modified plan was the one that formed the most famous engravings of the early plans for Washington DC that still survive. Everything that happened subsequently was based on Ellicot's plan, though it was all originally inspired by the awkward but brilliant Pierre Charles L'Enfant. L'Enfant's original triangle remained, as did his idea for a wide, central avenue leading west from the Capitol. The monument he had intended for George Washington was eventually built, though not in exactly the place he intended it to be.

This is the official story of how Washington DC came into existence, but we were to discover that there was much more going on in the mind of L'Enfant than meets the eye. Was Pierre Charles L'Enfant a Freemason? The short answer is that we don't know. But since George Washington was so keen on the Craft and since L'Enfant idolized Washington, it is likely that he was. It has to be remembered that L'Enfant had also served under the charismatic General Lafayette, who was certainly a Freemason. It doesn't really matter whether or not L'Enfant was himself a Freemason. What is definitely the case is that he was in possession of knowledge that was Freemasonic in nature, and he must also have been well versed in astronomy, as well as possessing information about a truly ancient measuring system that dated back to at least 4000 BC. (A full breakdown of the intended dimensions of Washington DC in Chapter 8 will demonstrate this.)

Undoubtedly, L'Enfant was also committed to building the 'City of the Goddess', which is what Washington DC would eventually be. It is unlikely that this was his own idea exclusively; it may have come directly from George Washington, but it is more likely to have been dreamed up by a committee, the composition of which is now lost to us – as it was always intended to be.

As we have seen, Andrew Ellicot also had a substantial part to play in the final dimensions and look of Washington DC. He did not change L'Enfant's plans too much, simply straightening a few roads and making a few other modifications to intersections, but he was heavily involved and was reported to have been relieved when it was possible for him to leave the area and get away from the political pressure of the job. Ellicot may also have been a Freemason. Indeed, David Ovason, author of *The Secret Zodiacs of Washington DC*, is convinced that he was. Ovason claims to have proof, but does not offer it because of a confidence he had given to a witness. In some ways it is unlikely that Andrew Ellicot would have been a Freemason, if only because he came from a long line of Quakers, who do not approve of Freemasonry. On the other hand, Ellicot readily took part in the War of Independence, and Quakers don't believe in fighting either.

Some criticism has fallen upon David Ovason for his assertion that this or that person who was present in the development of Washington DC must surely have been a Freemason, but I think this is less important than is sometimes suggested. It is my belief that Freemasonry contains the germ of the ancient knowledge that went into the creation of Washington DC and that knowing Freemasons may have become involved at least partly *because* of their membership in the Craft. However, what happened at the time betrays a deeper awareness and a greater understanding of a number of matters than the average Freemason would ever know. As a result I continue to believe that those who planned Washington DC, and who built into it so much of their own knowledge and beliefs, may or may not have been Freemasons. That they were *allied* to the Craft there is no doubt, but it is obvious that in the end Freemasonry served them, and not the other way round.

From first to last, almost everything associated with the planning and building of Washington DC shows a great awareness of Goddess-based religion, and this extends right back to the choice of the site.

The reader will recall that probably as a result of George Washington's influence, it was decided to place the new federal district half in Maryland and half in Virginia. If this was a coincidence, it was a fortuitous one because the names of both states are allied directly to the Goddess. Maryland was named after a British royal with the name Mary, but that does nothing to detract from the fact that Mary is the name of the mother of Jesus. The Virgin Mary stands at the centre of what might be termed a cult in the Catholic Church that places her at least on a par with God. In some ways I hesitate to call this a cult because it is so widespread in the Church. The Virgin Mary as a goddess might not be authorized Church dogma, but at a practical level it is a fact nevertheless.

Meanwhile Virginia, which originally was named after the virgin queen Elizabeth I of England, also carries a strong association with the Goddess, as indeed did Elizabeth herself to at least some of her courtiers. The virgin is also the name of the most important zodiac sign as far as Washington DC is concerned, and so placing the federal district at the intersection of two states with names such as these must have appeared to be, at the very least, the work of Providence. In reality the site may have been chosen in part *because of* the names the two states already had.

Congress stipulated that the boundary of the new territory should be no more than 10 miles square. By this they meant that none of its four boundaries must exceed 10 miles in length. The planners took Congress at its word and created a square, though with its points and not its flat sides facing the cardinal points of the compass, so that, when seen on a map, it has the look of a diamond. This is immediately noteworthy because as I have already observed the diamond is a particularly significant figure in terms of the feminine, and the Goddess in particular. How appropriate therefore that the votive offering made when the first boundary stone was put in place should have included corn and wine!

Right from the start the new district was referred to as Columbia – but why? The answer is simple, straightforward and unambiguous. Columbia is the name of a goddess and, what is more, a goddess specifically associated with the United States. How the name came into existence is a story in itself.

Back in the earliest days of the American colonies, discussions that took place in the British parliament could not be directly reported in newspapers – it was illegal. But by the 18th century, literacy was growing amongst the public of Britain and a developing intelligentsia wanted news of what Parliament was up to. Wits such as the political commentator, satirist and writer Jonathan Swift (1667–1745), thought up ways to get across to the public what was taking place in the House of Commons and the House of Lords by disguising it. Swift had written a thinly disguised piece of satire called *Gulliver's Travels*, which detailed the journeys of a hapless marooned sailor named Lemuel Gulliver, who found himself in all manner of strange lands, amongst giants, midgets and even a civilization run by horses.

The book was immensely successful, even when it was first written. As a result, when people commented in the press about British foreign policy as discussed in Parliament, they would use *Gulliver's Travels* as a storyline upon which to pass on the information. Discussion in the British Parliament was referred to, particularly in *The Gentleman's Magazine*, as 'Reports on the debates of the Senate of Lilliput' (Lilliput being the name of one of the countries the fictitious Gulliver had visited). It was in this context that the name Columbia occurred.

Columbia was the name used by *The Gentleman's Magazine* to refer to the American colonies. It has always been assumed, and still is in most circles, that the name Columbia was derived from the name of Christopher Columbus. Columbus is always credited as the discoverer of America (though millions of Native Americans would of course disagree). The word 'Columbia' may well have been first dreamed up by Samuel Johnson (1709–84), the brilliant British writer and lexicographer.

Most countries have a patron goddess, such as Britannia for Britain and Marianne for France, and the developing colonies in North America chose the name 'Columbia' for theirs. So it might appear that what at first began as a sort of joke ended up as a goddess – because that is precisely what Columbia became. But is it really that simple? In order to get at the real truth we need to chase the word Columbia back beyond the name of the Genoese mariner Columbus. Christopher's real surname was Colombo, which may originally have been derived from a place of origin. But the linguistic root of the word is the Latin Columbidae, which is the name of all the birds in the dove and pigeon family. In Italian the word for dove is 'Colombo', whilst in Latin it is 'Columba'.

Now things begin to get really interesting, because the dove has been associated with the Great Goddess since time out of mind. The reader will recall my description of the Minoan civilization of Crete. The Minoans were almost certainly representative of cultures that existed around them in the European Bronze Age. The reason they stand out is because they have inadvertently left us more evidence of their existence, lifestyle and beliefs than any other culture from such an early period. Although we are short on specifics regarding many elements of Minoan life, some things are known. Experts are quite convinced that Goddess worship reached a definite peak in Minoan Crete and there are certain facts associated with the Goddess of Crete that can be observed right across the rich veins of archaeology that exist on the island. One of these is the strong association between the Goddess of Crete and the dove. I have been aware of this connection ever since my own investigations into Crete began, and in many places on the island I have seen representations of the dove in locations where the Goddess was worshipped.

The *Encyclopedia Mythica* (online publication) says:

> Without doubt birds, and especially doves, played an important role in Minoan belief. According to a current interpretation, doves could be understood as embodiment (epiphany) of a divinity, a representation of a goddess in a bird form nearby her sacred place – a shrine or on a tree.

The reader will also recall that I made reference to the fact that physical representations of the Goddess are nonexistent in artefacts from Minoan Crete, though it is generally accepted that her presence was denoted by a pillar or pillars. In the Heraklion Museum on Crete there is a delightful model of a temple to the Goddess dating back to Minoan times. Like many shrines of its type it contains pillars and upon the pillars are carefully modelled doves. There are numerous other examples and, for this reason, the Goddess of Minoan Crete is often referred to as the 'Dove Goddess'.

Homer tells us that the Goddess was able to transform herself into a bird, and one of the personifications of the Greek goddess Aphrodite (Roman Venus) was a dove.

It may therefore come as no surprise to learn that the dove ultimately became important to Christianity. The dove had been important to Jewish devotees too. They had no goddess but the dove was one of the most sacred animals to be used as a sacrifice at the Temple in Jerusalem. However, it was not used in this way by Christians. From a very early date the dove became synonymous with the Holy Spirit, which is part of the all-important Trinity of Father, Son and Holy Spirit. In the New Testament the Holy Spirit is directly equated with the dove, which appeared as John the Baptist was about to baptize Jesus in the waters of the River Jordan.

There is no doubt that, to many devotees over the centuries, the Holy Spirit has had a *feminine* persona. In Greek it is called *Sophia*, which literally means wisdom, and it is no coincidence that Sophia went on to become a popular female name, though it is never used for men.

An entire book could be written about Sophia and what she has meant to theologians, philosophers and others over the centuries, but in a Christian mystical sense she was often called 'Virgin Sophia'. On a carving in Pennsylvania she is actually depicted with the wings of a dove, so the relationship between Sophia and the dove was certainly established in the United States at the very start of the 19th century, and almost certainly much earlier.

So we can see that in pagan religion, Christianity and even philosophy, the dove holds a central place. The dove can literally be the Goddess or

Figure 16. Depiction of the Virgin Sophia in Harmony, Pennsylvania, USA

it can be attributed to the feminine quality of Godhead: how appropriate then that the patron goddess of the United States is called 'Columbia'. To suggest that this came about by chance, or simply as a result of a satirist's joke, seems out of the question in view of all that followed. The name of the goddess was chosen very carefully, and the foundation of the capital of the United States was named in her honour. The city itself may be called Washington, but the all-important district of which it is a part is Columbia. It cannot therefore be denied that Washington DC is indeed the City of the Goddess. How appropriate such a designation is will become apparent as our story unfolds.

Meanwhile, the connection between Columbia and the Dove Goddess of ancient Minoan Crete may seem to be nothing more than a coincidence. I would call it coincidence myself, were it not for the fact that there is much more to connect Washington DC with a fabulous civilization that was destroyed by a natural disaster well over 3,000 years ago. What is more, both Washington DC and the district of which it is a part also have a strong connection with other Bronze Age cultures in Western Europe. We don't know much about Minoan abilities when it came to stargazing, except for the fact that the version of the zodiac we use these days almost certainly came from Crete. But we do know far more about the sky-watching abilities of people who were already building astronomically aligned monuments many centuries before Minoan Crete even existed. These cultures sprang up in Britain, the land that lay at the very foundation of the United States.

Author David Ovason has claimed that Washington DC is a city that owes its entire orientation and design to astronomy and astrology. Quite independently I came to more or less the same conclusions over a decade ago. It is now time to look at the sky above Washington DC.

CHAPTER FIVE

THE SKY OVER WASHINGTON

Astronomy, Geometry and City Planning

M en such as Benjamin Franklin and Thomas Jefferson, who were instrumental in the founding of the United States, were fascinated by science. Both had numerous interests in the scientific world but each was p rticularly keen on astronomy. This is not surprising because astronomy reached the zenith of development as the 18th century progressed.

Slowly but surely the planets on the outer edge of the solar system were being discovered, and men of letters were spending time looking more closely at the Moon, Mercury and Venus through telescopes that were improving and becoming more powerful with every passing decade. Both Franklin and Jefferson had telescopes of their own and would have relished the chance to view the Moon's craters or the strange markings on the surface of red Mars, but these new views of the cosmos came about at a point in history when the earlier legacy of astronomy was still widely respected.

For thousands of years humanity had accepted that nothing that happened above our heads in the sky was a random chance event, neither was it merely the natural sequence of planetary motion. Even the revered Isaac Newton, who taught us so much about gravity and planetary paths throughout the heavens, was a time-served astrologer. He believed, ardently and sincerely, that what happened in the sky could and did have a profound bearing on life here below.

This was not a new idea. As we have seen, our concept of the plane of the ecliptic being split into 12 equal sections, more or less, which we call the zodiac probably came about as much as 4,000 years ago in Crete. It was the profound belief of Professors Michael Ovenden and Archie Roy of Glasgow University that this was the case. They spent years looking at ancient poems and dealing with the precession of the equinoxes to establish where and when the zodiac we know today must have come about. The result, which is borne out in particular by an ancient poem known as 'The Phaenomena' by the Greek philosopher Aratus *c.* 310/15–240 BC, was that the zodiac must have come into use around 2600 BC and that it must have taken place at a latitude of about 36° north. The only culture that could have provided it at this latitude and during this period was the early Minoan Cretan civilization. Aratus, whose own poem was taken from an earlier source, specifically says that Father Zeus, the king of the Greek gods, was born in Crete (a legend that exists in other stories too) and that he set the zodiac's limits as a child.

My own work with the Minoan culture also indicates that the Minoans had a peerless understanding of Sun, Moon and planetary movements and that they had an accurate way of tracking the heavenly bodies across a sky they knew well how to divide.

Be that as it may, the Babylonians and Egyptians were also interested in astronomy but, apart from a growing fascination with numbers and a desire to subdivide the year more accurately, this ancient quest to understand the movements of the heavens was centred much more on astrology than on the astronomy that star- and planet-gazing eventually became. Astrology had to do with kingship in particular, and with seeking positive circumstances for waging war.

In the next chapter I intend to deal specifically with the tremendous importance of the neoclassical era that began in the late 17th century and continued throughout the 18th century, but briefly the idea developed with the era of the 'age of reason' that the ancient civilizations had something important to tell us. Archaeological discoveries in Greece and Turkey, but especially the finding of the ruins of Pompeii and Herculaneum in Italy, fascinated the ever thirsty 18th-century Western mind, while the new freedom of information, advances in printing and a new literacy made the ideas of the ancient philosophers available to anyone.

Far from being dismissed as nonsense, as it is by science these days, astrology was embraced by astronomers of the 18th century. The trade in almanacs and other books that professed to interpret heavenly happenings in terms of the part they must play in human affairs was brisk on both sides of the Atlantic. The appearance and development of semi-mystical associations, such as Freemasonry and Druidism, added to a heady mixture of ancient and modern possibilities, suffused together into a concoction that fed the minds of richer 18th-century gentlemen. They built neoclassical houses for themselves, and had engineers make grand and often huge telescopes that could be housed in ornamental observatories in their gardens. They became ever more conversant with ancient ideas about the zodiac, together with the meanings of planetary movement and the angles formed between planets and stars that it was generally assumed had a bearing on every aspect of earthbound life.

Freemasonry is filled with astronomical and astrological allegory. Much of this was demonstrated fully by Robert Hewitt Brown, a 19th-century American Freemasonic expert who wrote down his observations in a book called *Stellar Theology and Masonic Astronomy*. Hewitt Brown, who is still well respected as a Masonic investigator, subjected just about every ritual and symbol of Freemasonry to intense study and came to the conclusion that practically everything within the Craft is related in some way to the Sun, the Moon, the planets and the stars.

His book has now been republished, though I first came across it in a photocopied form taken from a copy of the book that had been kept in a Masonic library. In the photocopies I possessed, certain passages had been carefully erased, using a pen and ink. Fortunately for me the act of photocopying the pages had magically reinstated the printed words beneath, so I was able to read the passages quite easily. As I will presently show, the sections that someone had tried to keep from the eyes of his fellow Masons are quite telling.

Figure 17. The 'Beautiful' or 'Weeping' Virgin of the Third Degree

Hewitt Brown finds astronomy and astrology everywhere in Freemasonry but there is one enduring image that is important to United States Freemasonry in particular that he dealt with in great detail. This is an image associated with the Master Mason ceremony that is known as the 'Weeping Virgin of the Third Degree'.

This particular image, at least in the form we see it today, did not come into existence until early in the 19th century: it was first presented to American Freemasonry by a well-known Freemasonic lecturer named Jeremy L. Cross from New Hampshire, who had been born in 1783. Cross was an avid Freemason and wanted to bring together all the relevant symbols of the Craft in a book called *Hieroglyphic Monitor*. Cross believed that information relating to Freemasonry was much better learned and understood by Masons and prospective Masons if presented in this hiero-glyphic form, and it is true that drawings of this sort are still of the utmost importance in Freemasonic lodges.

The particular example of the Weeping/Beautiful Virgin is mentioned over several pages of explanation by Hewitt Brown in *Stellar Theology*. Hewitt Brown knew Jeremy Cross and learned from him at first hand how this hieroglyph came into existence. It becomes clear that the broken pillar, which represents an epitaph to the murdered Hiram Abif, was Cross's own invention, though Hewitt Brown has no idea where Cross got the idea for the weeping Virgin or any of the other components of the picture. The truth is that the hieroglyph is very telling, especially for anyone who understands astrology, astronomy and mythology.

The reader will notice that in this version of the hieroglyph right above the head of the beautiful Virgin is an astrological symbol. This is the recognized glyph for the zodiac sign of Virgo. The fact is emphasized by the sweep of the zodiac, which to the top left shows the glyph for Leo, and to the lower left that for Libra (the two zodiac signs that lie either side of Virgo). What is also quite obvious is the fact that Cross was well aware of

Figure 18. Alternative version of the Weeping or Beautiful Virgin of the Third Degree

the importance of Virgo to the time of the autumn equinox because it is during the build-up to this time that the Sun occupies this zodiac sign.

Figure 18 shows another version of the hieroglyph, this one containing some items that are not in the first, but also omitting some objects that are included in the version used by Robert Hewitt Brown.

The picture has been reversed here and the zodiacal information is completely missing. Two of Cross's intended features are present, these being a book on the broken pediment and an urn, held in the left hand of the Virgin. Freemasons are told that the broken pillar symbolizes Hiram Abif who, as we have already learned, was murdered by jealous stonemasons in the confines of the unfinished Temple of Solomon. The broken pillar represents the fact of his untimely demise. The open book is said to list Hiram's achievements and virtues, whilst the Virgin herself is represent ative of the Temple. The foliage she carries in her hand, Freemasons are told, is symbolic of a sprig of acacia that was said to have marked his temp- orary grave, whilst the figure in the background represents Time, which the aspiring Mason is told will heal wounds and bring everything to fruition.

This explanation is, like so many other explanations in Freemasonry, something of a fudge, and one would not have to be especially learned to see straight through it. Nevertheless, there is much more to the symbolism of the Weeping Virgin than almost all American Freemasons learn these days, and the whole is representative of what *really* lies at the heart of the Third Degree ceremony.

The Virgin is clearly intended to be Isis, the Egyptian goddess. The ancient tale of Isis and her husband Osiris relates that Osiris was murdered and sealed in a sarcophagus that was set adrift on the Nile. The coffin ultimately floated off to Byblos, where it lodged in the mud. It was ultimately incorporated into the trunk of a grand and magnificent tree, which the King of Byblos had cut down to make a pillar in his palace.

Isis searched diligently for her lost husband and she eventually found the pillar at the palace, which she broke apart to release the sarcophagus. The fact that the Virgin is weeping in the hieroglyph also identifies her as Isis, who is said to have wept constantly for her lost husband. In some versions of the story Isis was indeed a virgin and did not participate in a sexual act until after Osiris was found. Some say she created a phallus from beeswax, whilst others claim she was eventually fertilized by Osiris.

In Hewitt Brown's version of the hieroglyph we can see that the Virgin is holding foliage in her left hand and that it is appearing to cross the zodiac that passes overhead. This is symbolic of the harvest, which occurs at this time of the year, culminating around the date of the autumn equinox. The figure behind the Virgin is indeed Time, but also representative of the planet Saturn. In this picture he is there to indicate the passing year and the fact that the god who dies in the autumn, so that we might eat, will be resurrected in due season. It goes without saying that although this particular hieroglyph represents a telling of the Isis and Osiris corn myth, it is equally applicable to the Greek Demeter, whose own Mysteries were also celebrated at this part of the year – to coincide with the autumn equinox and the harvest.

There could be no better telling of what at least *some* Freemasons thought of the autumn equinox. Since this hieroglyph is used in connection with the Third Degree ceremony, in which the participating Freemason is symbolically murdered and resurrected, the symbolism of the Mystery religions and the dying corn god are entirely appropriate. Osiris was resurrected because of the love and dedication of Isis, whilst in the Greek myths Dionysus was brought back to life thanks to the intervention of Demeter. Both stories stem from an earlier myth that seems to have predominated back in the Neolithic period.

I have no doubt whatsoever that Robert Hewitt Brown, who wrote *Stellar Theology and Masonic Astronomy*, was fully in possession of all these facts and that he was under no misapprehension regarding the true intention of the Third Degree raising of the Mason. Neither was its significance lost on at least some future generations of Freemasons because in the original book from which my photocopies had been taken, all the deleted sections had either related to the story of Isis and Osiris or were connected with Virgo as the Great Goddess.

How appropriate it is, therefore, to see the importance of this particular time of year (the autumn equinox) for the planners and builders of Washington DC.

Another aspect of Freemasonic interest (one might even say obsession) in astronomy and astrology is revealed through something that is often used as a stick with which to beat the Craft. This is the reference, in some of the degrees of Scottish Rite Freemasonry, to Lucifer. Practically everyone of a Christian background who reads the name Lucifer will instantly equate it with the Devil. This is precisely what so many fundamentalist Christians do and there are many accusations made against Freemasonry, especially in websites, that the Craft serves the Devil and not God.

The reason that Christians have come to associate Lucifer with the Devil is because of a particular verse in the Old Testament. In the King James version of the Bible we can read in the Book of Isaiah, chapter 14, verse 12: '*How art thou fallen from heaven, O Lucifer, son of the morning! how art thou cut down to the ground, which didst weaken the nations.*'

This is the only place in the Old Testament in which the name of Lucifer appears, but it became associated within the Christian tradition that the Devil was once an angel, who fell from grace and was cast down by God, after which he became God's most implacable enemy.

It could be that those who draw this conclusion and who use it as a means of attacking Freemasonry will be surprised to hear that they have the whole thing about as wrong as is possible. Lucifer is not the Devil and never was. What is more, this particular verse of the Bible has nothing at all to do with the name *Lucifer*, except as a result of a faulty, though understandable, translation.

The name of the king in question roughly translates as 'light of the morning'. This whole part of Isaiah represents the Hebrews' hatred for the Babylonian king and this particular extract glories in the fact that no matter how great and powerful he might have been, he was eventually cut down by death, as all people are.

The authors of the King James Bible relied heavily on the 4th-century St Jerome, a man who translated the Bible into Latin. It was Jerome who took the name of the Babylonian king and rendered it as 'Lucifer'. The word Lucifer is Latin and means 'Morning Star' or 'Light Bringer'. This was probably as close as St Jerome could get to the real name of the Babylonian king, but the fact that he used a Latin name in the midst of a section that was obviously translated from the Greek gives ample proof that this name is *his* translation.

The name 'Lucifer' has no real Christian or Jewish pedigree at all before St Jerome used it. It is specifically used in Latin to describe the planet Venus as a morning star. Because the orbit of Venus lies inside that of the Earth, we can see two separate parts of its orbit. Venus, from our perspective, alternates between appearing in the morning, before the Sun rises, and in the evening, after the Sun has set. To Latin speakers Venus was 'Lucifer' when a morning star and as an evening star they usually referred to it by the Greek name 'Hesperus'.

The famous American Freemason, Albert Pike (1809–91), has been taken to task for well over a century on the subject of Lucifer because he was reported (as it turned out quite wrongly) as having suggested that Freemasons worship Lucifer (and therefore in the minds of Christians, the Devil). If he used the word at all he was referring to Venus or the path of light, and certainly not alluding to the Devil in any way.

John J. Robinson, researcher and writer, covered the subject extensively in his book *A Pilgrim's Path*.[10] He points out how surprised and shocked he was to discover that the verse in question had nothing to do with either the Devil or Lucifer. He cites it as just another example of the way Freemasonry is often attacked regarding matters that the attackers simply don't understand.

However, it remains a fact that Lucifer, and Venus generally, is of supreme importance to Freemasons. In some Masonic settings an illuminated five-pointed star represents part of the furnishings of a Masonic temple and is placed in the east (indeed it is the first thing the raised Third Degree Mason sees when his blindfold is removed). In other settings it is placed at the centre of the chequered floor of a Masonic temple. The emblem is known as 'The Blazing Star'.

Early astronomical interpretations of the Blazing Star, first mentioned in 1735, such as that by Robert Hewitt Brown, suggest that it is representative of the Sun; but this is unlikely since the Sun is used in other Masonic icons and symbols. What sets the Blazing Star apart is that it has five points, and this is what connects it specifically to the planet Venus. Unfortunately, and once again quite without any real justification, the five-pointed star or pentacle has also been associated with Satanism, when in reality it was once a regularly used Christian symbol.

For centuries five-pointed stars have been associated with Venus. This is explained in detail in my books *The Goddess, the Grail and the Lodge* and *The Virgin and the Pentacle*. This is because Venus and the Earth have a very special and unusual relationship. When seen from the Earth, Venus has an orbital cycle of 584 days. In reality, Venus orbits the Sun once every 224.7 days, but since the Earth is also travelling around the Sun at some speed, the period of Venus as seen from Earth appears to be considerably longer – we are observing Venus' movements from a moving observation platform.

It must have been obvious to the very first star-watchers that there was a direct connection between the observed cycle of Venus and that of the Earth year. For every eight Earth years, five Venus cycles can be observed. Indeed, if the true Earth year were exactly 365 days, this 8:5 relationship would be exact. In reality it is very slightly inexact, meaning that every 40 years there is a discrepancy of around two days. If the movements of Venus are plotted on a map of the sky over a 40-year period they produce a five-pointed star.

I have shown, both in this work and in my previous books, how important Venus was to our ancient ancestors but, since its cycles are still represented in Freemasonic symbols and the Blazing Star is often referred to as one of the most important symbols of the Craft, its presence acts as another forceful reminder of just how important astronomy is to the working principles of Freemasonry.

I have great respect for the American author David Ovason, whose own research into Washington DC has somewhat paralleled my own. In his book *The Secret Zodiacs of Washington DC*, he points out that the use of zodiac wheels in art, especially in sculpture and statuary, is totally out of proportion in Washington DC when compared with other places where neoclassical architecture sprang up around the same time. What is more, Ovason noted that in so many cases there was a specific reference in these zodiacs to the sign of Virgo. Ovason knows his astrology and his mythology well and asks the question: '*Can it be true that such esoteric bodies as the Masons regard these ancient gods and goddesses of the stellar pantheon as living beings, with the power to exude benefices and virtues on certain parts of the Earth?*'

It is a fair question and especially so when one bears in mind the laying of the cornerstone of the Capitol, an intended and obvious temple, at precisely the time of year when the Sun is in the zodiac sign of Virgo. If we take the Sun as representative of the male God and the sign of Virgo as the Goddess, then we can assume that it was considered that sexual congress took place between the pair during this part of the year. As with the Corn God myth, the old god died immediately after this congress took place. But the fruit of the union was the seed corn that was planted to ensure next year's crop.

Ovason claims that Pierre Charles L'Enfant's orientation of Pennsylvania Avenue, which runs southeast from the White House down to the Capitol, is part of the astronomical and astrological nature of Washington DC's orientation. He points out that if one were to stand at the Capitol on the day of the summer solstice (around 21 June) the setting Sun would shine right down Pennsylvania Avenue because the road was constructed with this annual event in mind – in other words the angles are the same. Broadly speaking this is true, since the Sun sets 17° north of west at Washington DC on the day of the summer solstice and Pennsylvania Avenue also has this angle as it runs northwest from the Capitol up towards the White House.

I don't think we really have to look any further than the orientation of the Mall itself to see what the planners of Washington DC had in mind in terms of astronomy – especially when we take this together with the placement of the Capitol. From the very start the Capitol was intended to be the most important structure in the new city. It was here that discussions would take place and where laws for the new country would be tabled and passed. This was genuinely intended to be a nation 'of the people, by the people and for the people'. There would be no king and everyone (apart from unfortunate black slaves and indigenous Americans) would have a part to play in the running of the country.

L'Enfant had originally intended a huge palace for the president's house, but this never came about, most probably because of the beliefs of some of the most important founding fathers such as George Washington and Thomas Jefferson. In their minds everything and everyone, including the president, was subservient to the will of government. The president, though clearly a figurehead, was just *one* of those people and as such he did not deserve to live in a sumptuous palace. As a result, the White House must be one of the more modest presidential homes in the world. Although Washington DC now has many grand and glorious buildings, none was ever intended to be quite as grand and glorious as the Capitol.

The Capitol sits at the top of a hill at the eastern end of the Mall. Anyone standing on the western steps of the Capitol can gaze west down the Mall towards the huge bulk of the Washington Monument. Originally this was intended to be a statue of George Washington on a horse (or at least that is what we are told). In reality, and as far as I can ascertain, though an equestrian statue may once have been postulated as part of the final structure, it was from first to last intended to be a tall, freestanding pillar.

Any real effort to create an epitaph to a man who was almost univer- sally respected in his lifetime and upon whose tireless effort the United

States depended so heavily in its first years, did not get moving until 1832, the centenary of George Washington's birth. The committee that collected donations and put out a statement of its intentions did not actually specify what the structure should look like, merely that it should be in keeping with the stature of the man it was meant to commemorate.

The project was put out as a competition, which was won by Robert Mills, a time-served architect who had previously built other monuments to celebrate the life of George Washington. Mills was a Freemason, and it showed in some of his work. As far as the intended monument in Washington DC was concerned he certainly did not fight shy of Masonic overtones.

Figure 19 shows what Mill's original design for the Washington Monument would have been like if it had been built the way he suggested. It was to be 600ft in height and would have had a central doorway surmounted by a winged sun, which is a typical Masonic icon. As can be seen in the picture, the obelisk that Mills proposed was to be surrounded by a colonnade, which in turn would carry the intended equestrian statue of George Washington.

It is said that the commissioners of the project balked at the proposed price tag of over one million dollars and that, as a result, they decided to proceed with the obelisk and leave the colonnade until a later time.

In practically everyone's comprehension an obelisk is self-evidently a *phallic* structure, and in the case of Egyptian obelisks the phallus is that of Ra, the Sun god. To a culture that virtually idolized phalluses the symbolism was quite intentional. Neither will this reasoning have been lost on Freemason Robert Mills.

As things turned out, the Washington Monument was not finished until after the American Civil War, and neither did it finally stand exactly where Pierre Charles L'Enfant had envisaged. It was meant to be on a direct east–west line from the centre of the Capitol, to be erected at a point at which a line running south from the White House would intersect the east–west line.

The site had been marked since the very beginning by a low, stone monolith, which became known as the Jefferson Pier. History relates that the project did not take place on this spot because the land there was considered unsafe for such a heavy monument and the Washington Monument actually rose from a spot 390ft east-southeast of the Jefferson Pier. I have personal doubts about the *real* reason for the Washington Monument being moved south of its original intended position and I don't think it had anything to do with unsafe ground. After all, the project

Figure 19. The Washington Monument as proposed by Freemason Robert Mills

was moved less than 400ft and it seems to me that the underlying topography is broadly similar across the full width of the Mall.

It is a little-known fact that the Mall does not truly run east–west, as was intended by L'Enfant. The buildings to the west of the Washington Monument, such as the Lincoln Memorial, were clearly sited so as to form a direct line from the Capitol through the Washington Monument and, as a result, the whole thing runs about 5° south of west. (The centre of the Lincoln Memorial should rightfully be 190ft north of where it actually is.) As we shall presently see, this spoiled L'Enfant's original right-angled triangle in terms of its intended overall length. Neither does the Washington Monument stand on the intended prime meridian of Washington DC that we will discuss in Chapter 8 .

If the Washington Monument had indeed been built where L'Enfant intended it to be, it would have caused a major problem. Since the Sun, at the time of both the spring equinox and the autumn equinox, rises due east and sets due west, sunset on these two crucial days of the year would have been obscured by the monument itself. These days there are extremely tall buildings in Rosslyn, the district immediately across the Potomac to the west of the Mall, but this would not have been the case until well into the 20th century. In my estimation the view of sunset from the Capitol at the time of the spring and autumn equinox during the latter part of the 18th century and throughout much of the 19th century would not have been obscured either by buildings or the great mass of the Washington Monument. Even now the view is generally good, with the skyscrapers of Rosslyn being so far away that they only rise a degree or two from the western horizon as seen from the Capitol.

Although the Sun does indeed rise due east and set due west on the equinoxes, it does not pass straight across the sky, over one's head. Rather, at Washington DC, it rises in the east and then climbs south as it rises to reach an altitude of about 53° in the south before swinging round to set in the west, which it approaches from the south. As the Sun sets in the west at the time of the autumn equinox it brings with it the apparently moving sky and also the constellation of Virgo.

Just as the Sun set in Washington DC when the city was being created, the star that made contact with the top of the Washington Monument would have been Gamma Virginis, better known as Porrima. Porrima is slightly unusual in that it does not have an Arabic name as so many stars do, but rather a Latin one. Porrima was the Roman goddess of prophecy. It was to Porrima that Roman women prayed at the time of childbirth, hoping for a successful birth and a prosperous and happy life for the forthcoming child.

At the opposite end of the year, at the spring equinox, Porrima also made contact with the top of the Washington Monument just before dawn as it dropped towards the west – this time without the Sun in attendance. With it came the whole constellation of Virgo, which was symbolically 'pierced' by the phallic Washington Monument as the spring Sun rose in the east behind the Capitol building.

All of this seems irrelevant or even potty when viewed with modern eyes, but such considerations were still accepted as being of great importance, even at the end of the 18th century.

There will be much more to say about astronomy and astrology as our story unfolds but it is worth finishing this chapter by pointing out that the Capitol building, facing due east, shares this orientation with two other buildings which will become important to our story. One of these is the long-demolished Temple of Solomon on the Temple Mount in Jerusalem and the other is that strange little Scottish building known as Rosslyn Chapel.

CHAPTER SIX

DAWN OF THE NEOCLASSICAL

Architecture and the Orientation of the Capitol

From the first moment I stood on the Mall in Washington DC and gazed around, east to the stately grandeur of the Capitol and west towards the Washington Monument and the Lincoln Memorial beyond, I have been captivated by the beauty of the city. Extreme care was and still is taken to ensure that anything built, in this part of Washington DC at least, is in keeping with the original intentions of its creators. Its beauty and symmetry mainly owe thanks to the style of building that was most popular during the 18th century, when Washington was planned.

Even towards the middle of the 18th century there was nothing especially unusual about educated people showing a reverence for the ancient. For a long time artists had tried to capture the styles of truly old paintings and indeed, right back to Roman times, there had been a reverence for what was already old in Greek art and culture before the rise of the Roman Empire. What set neoclassicism apart, beginning in around 1760, was the insistence on getting it right, coupled with an increasing ability to distinguish the various styles that had predominated in ancient Greece and Rome specifically.

This was a period when the wealthy were starting to take themselves off on 'grand tours'. People from the western fringes of Europe, especially Britain and France, wanted to know more about countries such as Italy and Greece. Those who could afford it would travel for weeks, months or years, partly to look at 'antiquity in the raw' and also to acquire works of art to adorn the new neoclassical houses that were starting to spring up as people tore down Tudor and Jacobean mansions to replace them with something more inspiring.

Although archaeology in the modern sense of the word had not begun in the middle of the 18th century, there were keen antiquarians – people whose methods of digging up the past would seem distinctly suspect by today's careful standards, but who nevertheless had a genuine interest in the distant past. This was made even more fascinating by the discovery, in 1738 and 1748 respectively, of the buried cities of Herculaneum and Pompeii in Italy. These had been destroyed by a volcanic eruption in ancient Roman times and much of everyday life had been buried in a sort of time capsule that is still being exposed today. Those embarking on the grand tour could not miss such opportunities, nor would they fail to visit Florence, Venice, Rome and all the other Italian cities from antiquity.

Greece was a little more difficult to get at since it was under Ottoman rule, but people could and did approach it, as well as visiting some of its outposts, such as those on Sicily and Cyprus.

At the same time came an interest in beauty in its most natural forms – albeit manipulated to provide the natural vistas the rich and landed wanted. The pastoral idyll and the Arcadian ideal were all the rage. A romanticism developed in which those with extensive grounds would pay masters of their craft to lay out stunning but simple vistas, replete with trees and acres of pasture. Sometimes they would employ people to act out the idyll, becoming shepherds and shepherdesses in an idealized landscape, similar to those beloved of artists such as Poussin, born at the end of the 16th century, who had concentrated on classical landscapes.

Artists, writers and poets responded to this turning away from the frilly, fancy Rococo style, an extension of the late Baroque period, to the cleaner, simpler, more technically inspired ancient styles of Greece and Rome. Columns shot up everywhere and distant hills sported fancy little temples and deliberately built ruins – all to please the sensibilities of those with a taste for the old.

A typical example of a neoclassical feast is the city of Bath in southern England. Originally a Roman spa and religious site, Bath remained a significant but fairly small market town until it suddenly became fashionable. A trend developed in the middle of the 18th century for imbibing sometimes foul-tasting spring-water that was believed to have curative and restorative properties. Such springs or spas were fairly common throughout Britain but Bath had something else. Anything ancient was suddenly worth looking at, and Bath had Roman remains, together with the finest surviving Roman baths anywhere in Britain. These revived the fortunes of a flagging Bath around the same time that colonists in the New World were starting to count the cost of all the taxes the British government imposed on them. A bevy of new and inspirational architects turned Bath into a neoclassical wonderland and, by so doing, created one of the most beautiful cities in Europe.

There were not many places in Western Europe, even in the middle of the 18th century, where architects and town planners could start out with a clean sheet and produce something that, at the time, was both truly ancient in its inspiration and yet unbelievably modern. In Bath the formerly rural hills around the old centre of the settlement soon became festooned with neoclassical mansions and grand terraces of houses. This makes Bath highly distinctive and, as we shall see, it has a close connection with Washington DC and so is relevant to our story.

The delving into the ancient past that took place from the middle of the 18th century had a marked effect on the mentality of many people. It was at this time that Freemasonry started to become ever more popular, together with its English companion Druidism. Both had appeared in at least a formal sense at the start of the 18th century and each became synthesized and sanitized to suit the sensibilities of their new members – even though both were substantially older in one form or another.

Grand houses, even ones that were not actually knocked down, began to sport classical porticos; roof lines were adorned with stone urns, statuary and classical mouldings; well-heeled young women put on pastoral dances and masques and everyone who was anyone showed themselves to be utterly enchanted with the clean white lines and deep carved key patterns of the neoclassical.

When we look at the new United States of America, just after it won its freedom from Britain in the middle of the 1780s, we find a culture suddenly bursting into reality and anxious to show itself to the world as being as good as any other. It is quite understandable therefore that it would try to produce for itself a capital city that was as clean, crisp and modern as any neoclassical location such as, for example, the almost contemporary city of Bath in England.

It is worth saying, since my critics will certainly do so, that Greek architecture and classical statuary were bound to be placed all over Washington DC at the end of the 18th century. To infer any other possibility is about as realistic as telling any trendy young woman from the mid-1960s that she should avoid wearing miniskirts at any cost. In 1793, neoclassical was the undoubted style and it was the one that everyone was determined to follow.

On the other hand, if a group of people came together with a clean sheet and endless acres of land to utilize, and if that group was determined to build a city dedicated to a truly ancient goddess, they could hardly have chosen a period better than the end of the 18th century to do it. They could get away with just about anything, and all without arousing suspicion that anything unusual or untoward was taking place.

As an example, let us look at the statue on top of the dome of the Capitol. She is a majestic lady indeed because she stands 19ft 6in in her sandalled feet and weighs in at 15,000lbs. This statue is called 'Freedom, Triumphant in War and Peace'. Although she symbolizes everything I have come to learn about Washington DC and its creation, she did not actually come to stand on the Capitol dome until 1863. The Capitol was built in stages and it took a long time, but also the American Civil War got in the way of the project.

It is hard to imagine the iconic cast-iron dome of the Capitol without its splendid statue, even though her presence there puts to rest any doubt regarding what the building beneath her feet actually is. We simply take for granted that she is there and put her presence down to a fascination for the neoclassical, which was still grinding on in the middle of the 19th century.

The idea for a colossal goddess statue for the dome came from its architect, Thomas U. Walter, who, surprise, surprise, was a Freemason. He had wanted to call the statue 'Liberty'. Maybe it was because of Thomas U. Walter that the sculptor Thomas Crawford who, it is reported, but not proven, was another Freemason, decided to give his statue the famous 'Liberty Cap' that in a moment will take us to another relative of the goddess Freedom. The idea for the Liberty, or more properly Phrygian, cap did not go down well in some departments and so the statue ended up with a military style helmet surmounted by feathers.

It may seem like a moot point to call the statue 'Freedom' rather than 'Liberty' because both words mean more or less the same thing. However, there is a difference. Freedom is a concept, whereas Liberty actually was the name of a goddess, whose Latinized name was Libertas. Libertas was tremendously popular in ancient Rome and had a particular affiliation with freed slaves. In classical sculpture she is always seen wearing the

Phrygian cap, the same cap worn by revolutionaries at the time of the French Revolution.

The reason that the statue on the Capitol is called 'Freedom' and not 'Liberty' is because the senator in charge of the Capitol building at the time was none other than Jefferson Davis, who would eventually become the president of the Confederacy during the American Civil War. One imagines that freed slaves were not something close to his heart, and this alone may account for the missing Phrygian cap.

'Liberty' was the cry of the disgruntled colonists in British-owned North America when they complained about 'no taxation without representation', and it was also shouted long and hard in revolutionary France, with which the colonies in America had much in common.

'Liberty' is derived from the Latin word for pouring, as for example wine. Modern etymologists suggest that this is because the feeling of liberty is akin to the sensation of being drunk.

Deriving from early Roman times, Liberty, or more properly Libertas, was an important deity. Her origins probably lay in another goddess, part of the ancient Etruscan and Sabian pantheon. Her name was Feronia and she was the goddess of the dawn. Feronia was also a goddess of the earth and is directly associated with Mania, another Etruscan earth goddess. According to some modern sources, Feronia, and therefore Liberty, can both be seen as merely alternative representations of Persephone, who in turn is synonymous with her mother Demeter and also the Egyptian Isis.

If anyone doubts that the goddess Liberty is alive and well in the United States they merely have to take a trip to New York, where one of the largest statues ever created still guards the harbour. The Statue of Liberty is merely another representation of the same deity that watches over the Capitol. Both owe their existence to the rise and continued popularity of the neo-classical movement in art and architecture.

In reality there are statues of the Goddess all over historic Washington

DC. They are to be seen on countless epitaphs and are represented at practically every intersection, square and circle throughout the original city. In a week-long excursion to identify representations of the Goddess in Washington DC, I lost count of how many examples there are, but it must run into hundreds. Once again the criticism will be 'But there is nothing strange about that. Goddesses of one form or another are an integral part of neoclassicism and can be found everywhere.' In a way, this is the point I am making. If there is an influential but small section of society that secretly embraces Goddess worship, they can have a tremendous bearing on what art forms are used and this was certainly true at the end of the 18th century and throughout much of the 19th century.

It is an oft-quoted adage, but nevertheless true, that the best way to conceal almost anything is to 'hide it in plain sight'. I find it a sterling test to imagine what an alien might think if they were to be set down on our planet, to walk about and to make simple observations. Earlier in the book I used this alien idea when talking about the churches of Malta, and came to the conclusion that there are so many representations of the Virgin Mary in Malta's 365 churches that the alien visitor must surely arrive at the conclusion that the primary religion of Malta was one based on a predominant female deity.

If we now moved our alien to Washington DC and allowed him to roam around for a couple of days he would surely arrive at the conclusion that his previous assumptions were born out absolutely, and if he knew the purpose of the grand building on the hill, the Capitol, with its patron goddess high on the dome, he would probably return to his home planet convinced that the same goddess that ruled religion also had a strong part to play in the running of the state.

The same icon can have totally different meanings to different people. In Troyes Cathedral in Champagne, France, there is a beautiful representation of the Virgin Mary. In her crooked arm she carries a sheaf of wheat.

Away in England, in the hall of a magnificent mansion known as Castle Howard, is a Roman statue of the goddess Ceres (Roman counterpart of the Greek Demeter). The statue of Ceres is almost identical to the statue of the Virgin Mary in Troyes Cathedral, to the extent that they could be quite easily swapped around. To one person, both of these statues could represent Mary, the mother of Jesus, whilst to another observer they could both be the Roman Ceres or the Greek Demeter. A third person might simply assume that they were wonderfully executed representations of the female human form. It all depends on one's point of view, upbringing and knowledge.

Bearing this in mind, if we now spend a few days strolling around the city of Washington DC, and put ourselves into the mindset of someone to whom the Great Goddess of ancient times is still a hard-and-fast reality, we will see the entire city in a new and quite different light. So much of what we may have seen a thousand times before will now begin to make greater sense.

In itself this is proof of nothing. Evidence does not usually represent a single strand but rather many strands, braided together in such a way that it makes a strong and quite obvious rope. At this point in our story I have to willingly hold up my hands and say that the case for Goddess reverence on the part of at least some of the most influential of the Founding Fathers is a possibility, but it is certainly not proven. This is how Washington DC remained in my mind for many years, until what amounts to a random discovery changed everything.

CHAPTER SEVEN

THE BACKGROUND

Ancient Calendars and Measuring Systems

Thereis something surprising about Washington DC and the way it was planned and laid out. It might seem odd but, if we want to fully understand what turned out to be one of the greatest surprises of my life, we have to go back in time to a period long before anyone in the western hemisphere even knew of the existence of the American continent. What follows might seem at first to be something of a departure but it is essential to a full understanding of the true, staggering implications of Washington DC's planning.

It is now nearly 25 years since I first decided to take a short holiday on the island of Crete. I thought it might be fun to take a look at the Minoans, that mysterious, lost super-civilization about which, at the time, I knew very little.

One day into my vacation I came across something that would change my life forever. I saw it in a gift shop window. It was a picture of a baked clay disc, upon which was an incised spiral and many mysterious hieroglyphics set within groups. I stood and stared at the picture, before eventually going into the shop to purchase it.

Back at my hotel I was sitting on the terrace and looking at the photograph when the friendly proprietor happened to walk by. He stopped and we got into conversation. He told me what he knew about the disc, saying it had been discovered in the ruins of one of the Minoan palaces in the south of the island, which is how it had acquired its name, the Phaistos Disc. He also told me that I was looking at only one side of the disc. It was double-sided, he informed me, and the two sides were different.

Early the next morning this amazing man turned up at breakfast time with a perfect facsimile of the Phaistos Disc, which he presented to me. This is still one of my most prized possessions. George wouldn't take any money for the disc and, as generous as Cretan people are, he merely hoped that I would find it interesting. This was an understatement, and it certainly set the seal on my holiday because I determined to discover as much as I possibly could about both the Phaistos Disc and the culture that had created it.

I already knew quite a lot about ancient astronomy and it did not take me long to see in the two sides of the Phaistos Disc the matrix of a useful calendar. I knew it was a waste of time to try and interpret the linguistic meaning of the hieroglyphics on the disc because these have been a puzzle to the brightest and best linguistic experts ever since the Phaistos Disc was first discovered. The language spoken by the Minoans is not known and neither is it entirely certain in what way the hieroglyphics are meant to be read. Are they symbolic of individual words or do they represent phonetic components within a language?

Although I could not read the hieroglyphics, I could certainly count them. There were 123 hieroglyphics on side A of the disc, within 31 groups, and 119 hieroglyphics on side B of the disc, within 30 groups, and these facts almost immediately began to make sense to me.

People have been trying to formulate accurate calendars for tens of thousands of years. Etched bone plaques, from many different sites, have been found that are clearly intended to be lunar or solar calendars, and some of these are incredibly old. The need to track the year accurately

Figure 20. Reconstruction of Phaistos Disc Side A
Figure 21. Reconstruction of Phaistos Disc Side B

is understandable. It is especially important for farmers, who need to understand the seasons for planting, but also significant to hunter-gatherers, who are probably nomadic and need to be up to speed on the migration of prey species.

Unfortunately, the Earth year is not at all easy to deal with. There are two or three different sorts of year, dependent on what astronomical criterion is used to measure the year – and the year does not resolve to an even number of days. The sidereal year, judged by the apparent return of the Earth to its starting point in space since the year before, is 365.2564 days in length, whereas the tropical year, measured bearing in mind the fact that the Earth 'wobbles' on its axis, which has a bearing on the year's length, is 365.2422 days in length. Neither is particularly helpful and unless some way is discovered to deal with the year in a round number of days, to make the necessary compensations, within a few decades any calendar is going to get into a hopeless and ultimately useless muddle.

Humanity has devised many different ways to deal with this problem. In the modern age we judge the year to be 365 days in length, but we make compensations by adding an extra leap day every four years, and by making other compensations during century years. This keeps things more or less on track but even our modern method is not without its problems. Fortunately, such is our technical expertise these days that we can easily put things right.

Some ancient cultures celebrated a year of 360 days, comprised of 12 months of 30 days, with five extra days being added at the end of the year. Others stuck to 360 days and simply added an extra month when necessary, but few ancient civilizations had a truly accurate calendar, and even our own Western system fell into a terrible muddle after the Roman calendar started to go wrong in the Middle Ages. Eventually the whole thing needed to be recomputed and 10 full days were removed from the calendar to get things running more or less right again.

What I discovered in the number systems used on the Phaistos Disc was a method of rectifying the calendar that was extremely accurate and also incredibly simple. The breakdown of how I arrived at my conclusions can be found in my book *The Bronze Age Computer Disc* but, briefly, it occurred to me that the Minoans had used a ritual year of 366 days, comprised of 12 months of alternating 31 and 30 days in length. (The remnants of such months remain in our own calendar.) But the really ingenious part of the process was that the Minoans also had a second calendar, this time composed of 119 cycles of 123 days.

The two calendars ran alongside each other. The 123-day cycles were tracked on side A of the disc, with each hieroglyph representing 1 day, and the 119 'returns' of this cycle were tracked on side B of the Disc, with each hieroglyph representing a full 123-day cycle.

The Phaistos Disc runs for 40 years. After every four of the 123-day cycles, 1 day was removed from the ritual 366-day calendar. At the end of the 40 years, 3 extra days were added to the ritual calendar and these are shown as three dots at the end of the spiral on side A of the disc. It could hardly be simpler and, if the procedure is followed properly, the inaccuracy of the ritual Minoan calendar over the true sidereal year will never be more than 26 seconds of time in any year. This means that no other alteration would have to be made to the calendar, other than the ones specified in the system, for well over 3,300 years, which is a phenomenal achievement – longer than the survival of most civilizations.

All the numbers necessary to build and track this 366-day calendar, and to compensate so that it did not fall out of line with the *real* Earth year, were to be found on the Phaistos Disc, with each hieroglyphic representing one digit. Despite the fact that my idea did not exactly set the worlds of archaeology and history alight, I consoled myself with the thought that if I was wrong I had accidentally stumbled across the most ingenious calendar rectification system ever created.

As it turned out, the research of Professors Ovenden and Roy from Glasgow University regarding where and when the zodiac was first created were born out by my own investigations. There is an ingenious shorthand way of using the Phaistos Disc that relates specifically to the way the heavens are split by the zodiac. What is more, once again using the zodiac as the 'reference map' of the heavens, the same numbers employed by the Phaistos Disc to deal with the calendar can also be used to track the position within the zodiac of the Sun, Mercury and Venus at any time, on any day. The level of accuracy is breathtaking and this makes the Phaistos Disc – or at least the number bases that it contains – into a multifunctioning calculating machine of great simplicity but stunning accuracy.

The Phaistos Disc alone could be used to regulate the calendar, but when applied to the zodiac wheel it could do infinitely more. This seemed to me to be proof that the zodiac as we know it today was first laid down within the cool interiors of the Minoan palaces at about the same time the Phaistos Disc was created – probably around 2000 BC.

I was satisfied enough with my discoveries but also painfully aware that I had probably managed only to scratch the surface in terms of understanding what else the Phaistos Disc could do – and all without understanding a word of what it 'said'. I recognized that the Phaistos Disc itself might be only an *adjunct* to the systems it implied, and I was very sad that archaeologists had not located other discs of the same type. I remain convinced that the Phaistos Disc is only one of a whole family of discs used for a wealth of astronomical purposes in Minoan Crete.

The discovery of a calendar that allowed for 366 days in the Earth year fascinated me, and I began to explore what this might mean for developing mathematics and geometry. Then I met Christopher Knight. Together with a colleague, Robert Lomas, Chris had published a book called *The Hiram Key*, which up to that time was the most complete investigation of the true history of Freemasonry ever undertaken. The book proved to be immensely popular and somewhere within its pages I recognized a commonality with my own work. As a result, I arranged to meet Chris Knight and Robert Lomas and a period of co-operation began.

During my Minoan research I discovered that a Canadian archaeologist by the name of J. Walter Graham had been trying to establish what system of measures the Minoans may have used. By carefully measuring the remains of the various Minoan palaces, Graham was able to extrapolate that the Minoans had used a unit he called the 'Minoan Foot', extremely close in size to the modern standard foot, being only very slightly shorter. Graham's ideas were not universally accepted at first, until a previously unknown palace, Zakro, was unearthed after his initial research had taken place. Graham had, of course, never had access to this palace, but his estimation of the Minoan Foot fitted its dimensions perfectly, so his theory was proven.

Meanwhile, I was also fascinated by ancient measuring systems and there was one in particular that I knew well. It related to hundreds of standing stone circles, stone avenues and other structures from the Late Stone Age and Bronze Age in the British Isles and parts of France: this measuring system had been found, almost accidentally, by a Scottish engineer named Alexander Thom.

After the Second World War Thom became a professor of engineering at Oxford University. He was well respected and a stickler for exactitude. But he was also a man who revelled in history and astronomy. As a young man Thom had a hunch that many of the stone circles, especially in Scotland, had been used to track the Moon on its tortuous path and, in order to discover whether this was indeed the case, he set out, in his spare time, to measure as accurately as possible as many stone circles, avenues and the like as he could.

Thom surveyed hundreds of sites, from Orkney in the north down through Britain to Brittany in France in the south. He proved his theory

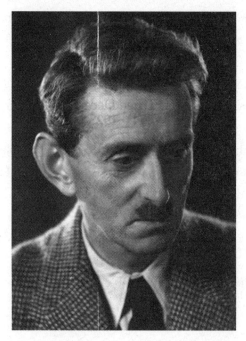

Figure 22. Alexander Thom

quite easily, and for that he is often referred to as 'the father of astro-archaeology', but he made another discovery which did not go down as well and which remains contentious in some circles to this very day.

As a result of his extremely careful surveying, Thom became aware that virtually all the sites he investigated had been planned and construct-ed using a single unit of linear measurement. This, Thom suggested, was 82.966cm in length (2.722ft) and he christened it the 'Megalithic Yard' (MY). To say that experts were sceptical is an understatement. They wanted to know how such a primitive culture as that inhabiting Britain 4,000 to 5,000 years ago could possibly have utilized a standard unit of measurement and kept it accurate, to an incredible degree, across such a wide geographi-cal area and for 2,000 to 3,000 years. Alexander Thom had no answer, but the data kept piling in. Nobody has ever suggested that Thom's surveying skills were suspect or that he was ever anything other than meticulous in the way he went about his work.

Thom also suggested that other standard units had been used. These were the Megalithic Rod, which was 2.5 times the length of the Megalithic Yard, and also the Megalithic Inch, of which he suggested there were 40 to the Megalithic Yard and therefore 100 in the Megalithic Rod.

By the time I was finishing *The Bronze Age Computer Disc*, I was starting to realize that the 366-day year celebrated by the Minoans was almost certainly part of something much bigger and more complex. I began to suspect that the very foundation of geometry had been quite different to what most mathematicians believed. These days geometry relies on circles of 360°. This has been the case for so long that it is automatically accepted that there is no other way to measure circles and angles, but this does not have to be the case.

Nobody could tell me where the 360° circle had originated, but it seemed to me that 360 was so close to the number of days in an Earth year that there must be a connection. Such a connection would be logical because the year is indeed a circle – the circle made by the Earth around the Sun. (The orbit of the Earth around the Sun is not a circle but rather an ellipse, but the fact is academic in terms of naked-eye astronomy.)

I now know the answer to where the 360° circle originated because we eventually worked it out. It did not originate in the path of the Earth around the Sun but rather that of the Moon around the Earth – *see* Appendices One and Two. (The 360° circle was created by the Sumerians and it relates to the period from one full moon to the next, which they rounded up to 30 days. The degrees of the circle are represented by the hours that elapse on Earth during this period. The Sumerians only had 12 hours in a day.)

I began to wonder whether the first geometry used by our ancestors had been slightly different and whether or not there had once been 366° to a circle. This seems odd to us today but it would be quite logical because each day of the year would then represent one degree of the great circle of heaven. Chris Knight and I began to look at the possibility and together we reached some startling conclusions. We discovered that if 366° geometry was used, and if the polar circumference of the Earth itself was considered to be a circle, some amazing things happened.

The story of our deductions is quite long but, in a nutshell, we discovered that if the Megalithic Yard (MY), rediscovered by Alexander Thom, was applied to a 366° geometry for the world, it would become a truly geodetic unit. In other words it would fit the polar circumference of the Earth in a very rational and quite obviously intentional way.

We are accustomed, thanks to the Sumerians, to having circles in which each of the 360° can be split into 60' (minutes) of arc and each minute of arc into 60" (seconds) of arc. The ancient system we rediscovered was slightly different. In this case each of the 366° were split into 60' of arc, but each minute was split into only 6" of arc. If this were done, the second of arc achieved, in terms of the polar circumference of the Earth, would measure *exactly* 366MY!

This was hardly likely to be a coincidence. What it amounted to was this: the length of the Megalithic Yard, multiplied by 366, then 360 and finally by 366 again, equals the polar circumference of the Earth. The result, starting out with Thom's Megalithic Yard of 82.966cm, is 40,009km, which is as near to being a true size for the polar Earth as makes no difference.

A further discovery, and one that really shocked us, was the realization that 366 Megalithic Yards is exactly the same thing as 1,000 Minoan Feet. Both equal 303.655 metres. It began to look as though the Minoans had used the same geometry as the Megalithic peoples of the far west of Europe, but had maintained a different basic unit of linear measurement – probably because of their domestic building needs, which were quite different from anything that took place in Stone Age or Bronze Age Britain.

But we were still faced with a basic problem. Experts would not accept the validity of the Megalithic Yard because it varied so little between sites where Thom said it had been used. Thom said it had been employed in the late Stone Age, at which time there was no metal to make 'primary' rods, which could be passed from site to site. Ropes would have been hopeless, as indeed would anything made out of any other organic material such as wood. Locally, the length of the Megalithic Yard could be scratched into stone, but this could hardly be transported across such a wide area – even assuming that there had been a degree of cohesion within society as a whole that could make such a thing possible.

It was because of these problems that Chris, Robert Lomas and I eventually realized that if it was indeed going to stay so incredibly accurate from site to site, there had to be some way to 'create' the Megalithic Yard wherever it was needed. We knew there was nothing in the natural world that is always the same. Units taken from arm length or foot length vary tremendously, so where could we find something that always remained the same and which could be accurately measured whenever it proved to be necessary?

The answer lay in the turning Earth itself. The Earth turns at a known and a consistent rate and, if that fact could somehow be utilized, an unchanging and accurate unit of linear length could be established. It was at this stage that we hit upon the pendulum.

A pendulum is, at its most simple, just a weight on a piece of twine, but it does have certain characteristics. A pendulum of a given length will always beat out the same period of time, whether it is swinging quickly or slowly. This might seem counter-intuitive but it is a fact. The only things that govern the rate of swing of the pendulum are the length of its string and the force of gravity, which to all intents and purposes is constant. (Actually gravity does vary slightly across the surface of our planet, dependent on latitude and height above sea level, but across the area where the Megalithic Yard was used it varies by an insignificant amount.)

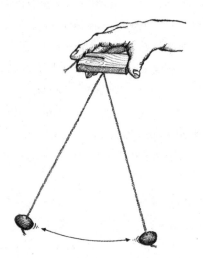

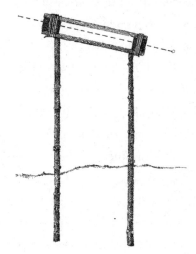

Figure 23. A simple pendulum. Not only is this an excellent and constant time-keeper, it is also a way of turning the passage of time into a known and replicable linear length.

Figure 24. A simple, braced wooden frame of the type used to observe Venus crossing one Megalithic degree of the heavens, whilst keeping track of the time with a swinging pendulum

It took a while to work it out but what we eventually discovered was that a pendulum that would swing back and forth 366 times during the passage of a star across one Megalithic degree of the horizon, would have a string length of exactly ½ MY. The computation worked well, but it wasn't *absolutely* accurate. Chris and I later went on to realize that only one heavenly body could set the size of the Megalithic pendulum *totally* accurately and it wasn't a star at all. It was the planet Venus, the speed of which, during a specific part of its orbit, provides the perfect setting mechanism for the pendulum length. Setting out a braced wooden frame on the horizon to track Venus across one Megalithic degree of the sky is easy and, if done correctly, the result will always be the same.

So it turned out that no standard measure for the Megalithic Yard ever needed to be made. The unit was simply reconstructed wherever it was required, and it was guaranteed always to be the same to within the tiniest fraction. Double the pendulum length was a true Megalithic Yard, which was used entirely accurately for countless centuries in Britain and parts of France.

Alexander Thom, one of the most patient and painstaking individuals ever to undertake research into our ancient ancestors, was fully vindicated. His findings were correct and the 50 years of his life it had taken him to collect them were not wasted. (For more information about the Megalithic system of measurements *see* Appendix One.)

It is worth noting again at this point that the only heavenly body that can be used to make the true and incredibly accurate Megalithic Yard is Venus, which the reader will doubtless recall is the planet of the Goddess. This will become relevant later.

Chris Knight and I decided to write a new book together, in which all our findings could be incorporated. It was called *Civilization One* and it detailed much more than the method for establishing a Megalithic Yard. We eventually realized that practically every measuring system used in the world today developed either from the Megalithic system, or was devised in an identical way, using a pendulum and a defined period of time.

This did not simply include linear measurement because the linear measurements themselves, in the form of cubes with sides of a known length, were used to create vessels for measuring the capacity of water, and the water in those cubes was used as a standard for weight measurements. The same system was used to create the litre and the kilogram from the metre, only 200 years ago. As a point of interest, the metric system was not new when the French claimed to have created it at the end of the 18th century: it had first been used in almost exactly the same form by the ancient Sumerians (*see* Appendix Two).

This meant that the Megalithic Yard was used to create an integrated measuring system that incorporated distance, time, volume and mass, all inextricably linked together and all tied directly into the physical dimensions of the Earth. The integrated Megalithic measuring system was positively stunning and, in terms of mass, it dealt in a concise way with everything from the weight of a barley seed, right up to the mass of the Earth itself.

So far reaching are the implications of our discoveries that orthodox science and archaeology are having some difficulty in coming to terms with them. Not a single criticism regarding our mathematics has ever been levelled and no expert has ever directly told us that we are wrong in any of our findings or statements. All the same, it takes a long time for ideas to change, and there is as yet no sign of our findings being taught in schools or universities. This is hardly surprising because to do so would involve some sort of explanation as to how so-called 'primitive' people could have known the size and even the mass of the Earth.

Chris and I were very happy with our findings, but there were a couple of facts that disappointed us. We had fully expected to find structures such as stone circles that incorporated a linear length of 366MY, because this would prove our thesis absolutely. Of course, 366MY is also one Megalithic Second of the Earth's polar circumference. Unfortunately, until well after we had written *Civilization One* no such measurement appeared and we began to think that we had got something wrong, or that maybe any such structure had not survived the ravages of time. When the truth finally came along we were stunned to realize that the reason we had not found the 366MY measurement was because the structures we had been studying were too new!

I saw a TV documentary about the English city of Bath. The narrator was talking about a particular structure in Bath – a circular block of regency terrace houses in neoclassical style, around a grassed central circus. The structure is called King's Circus, and it was designed by the architect John Wood and completed towards the end of the 1760s. What drew my attention was when the narrator suggested that the distance across the Circus, from the front of the houses, was just over 96 metres (around 317ft). I knew from past experience that this must mean the circumference of the structure would be in the region of 303 metres (about 996ft), and that meant its circumference was extremely close to 366MY.

At the first possible opportunity my wife and I set off to Bath, taking extremely long tapes and laser measuring instruments. It didn't take us long to discover that the narrator of the documentary was right. King's Circus in Bath has a circumference, at the front of its houses, of an almost exact 366MY.

When I did some research into the architect of this spectacular structure I discovered that he was a man obsessed with Freemasonry and Druidism and that he was particularly interested in the ancient stone circles of the area around where he lived. One of these was Stonehenge. John Wood had undertaken an in-depth study of Stonehenge and had measured it carefully.

I now went back to my earlier work and to Google Earth. All the measurements we had for Stonehenge related to the distances between the stones. What we had never measured was the henge itself. A henge is a circular ditch and bank. Henges are generally older than stone circles but, in the case of Stonehenge, the stones were arranged within an existing henge. To my absolute delight, the henge at Stonehenge has a circumference of 366MY, or one Megalithic Second of the Earth's polar circumference.

Now we had been introduced to the size significance of henges there was no stopping us. We found henges all over the place that conformed to our earlier predictions. In particular there were extremely large henges close to our own homes in the north of England. Three of these remain more or less intact and are known as the Thornborough Henges. They lie close to the town of Ripon in North Yorkshire, in northeastern England.

Each of the Thornborough Henges is so large that it would be possible to put London's St Paul's Cathedral into one easily. The three Thornborough Henges are all the same size and are known as type IIA henges, because each has two entrances. These henges are all twice as big as Stonehenge, with an outer circumference of 732MY (2×366). They are arranged in a row, running roughly from northeast to southwest.

At a stroke, our realization regarding the huge henges at Thornborough also bore out another prophecy we had made in *Civilization One*. We were aware that these ancient people knew a lot about circles and were fascinated by their dimensions. We expected to find circles with circumferences of 732 units because such a circle must have a diameter of 233 of the same units. It is very rare to find a circle in which both the diameter and the circumference can be measured in whole numbers of the same unit.

This is because the relationship between the diameter of a circle and its circumference is dependent upon *pi* (π), which is not a whole number but rather something approaching 3.14159. To get the circumference of a circle it is necessary to multiply the diameter by 3.14159. This is why the sort of circles we called 'pi survivors' are so rare – circles that could be measured in such a way that the diameter and the circumference came out as whole numbers of the same linear unit. Nevertheless, with their fascination for both the Megalithic measuring system and circles in general we estimated that our ancient ancestors would surely have hit upon this example, particularly since it involved the number 732, which is of course twice 366.

The discovery of these henges led to another shared book, called *Before the Pyramids*. Our work at Thornborough connected us to cosmology, and in particular to the constellation of stars known as Orion's Belt. Thornborough Henges are a copy on the ground of the three stars of Orion's Belt and the henge array is also connected in a very strange but provable way to the three most significant pyramids on the Giza Plateau in Egypt.

Thornborough Henges, and in fact all the henges that conform to the Megalithic pattern, were created around 3500 BC, so they are truly ancient. We are certain that they were used as naked-eye observatories and, together with an engineer in Northern Ireland, we have started to show how the sites were used. Many of the methods and measurements used in the Megalithic system could have been devised in research facilities such as Thornborough, which were undoubtedly religious as well as scientific sites, because in those remote times science and religion were more or less the same thing.

We were left with a specific puzzle. Had John Wood, the designer of King's Circus in Bath, known about the existence of the Megalithic Yard, or had he simply copied the dimensions of the henge at Stonehenge without realizing what he was doing? As far as we could tell, the King's Circus was the only relatively modern use of the Megalithic Yard, so it was very significant.

John Wood was a strange and enigmatic person. He had very particular ideas about prehistory and he delighted in covering the houses he designed with Freemasonic and Druidic iconography. We decided that if anyone at this point in history could possibly have known about the ancient Megalithic Yard and therefore Megalithic 366° geometry, it might easily be the charismatic John Wood. We also found other sites created by him in Bath that seemed to have a Megalithic resonance, but unfortunately John Wood did not live a long life and was not able to complete as many buildings in Bath as he had hoped.

The time had come to look elsewhere because we simply had to know whether knowledge of this ancient and absolutely brilliant system of geometry and measurement had somehow survived. We had long suspected that an ancient lineage had survived with specific beliefs and practices but in our wildest dreams we never expected to find a linear measurement being used in the 18th century that disappeared not long after 2000 BC.

So where could we go to find a large number of grand buildings that were created from scratch at the end of the 18th century and where we might be expected to find a good sprinkling of Freemasons and others interested in esoteric subjects? It didn't take long to work it out. We needed to look at Washington DC. True, we had no real expectation of finding anything significant, but once again we were going to be blown away by what we discovered.

CHAPTER EIGHT

ALMOST TOO INCREDIBLE FOR WORDS

Alignments and Proportions in Washington DC

At the time I was busy with something else, so Chris was the first of us to turn his attention to Washington DC. I got a phone call from him early one Monday morning. He was laughing.

'I've just found a henge in Washington DC,' he told me.

I knew this could not be the case. Henges are a peculiarly British structure, and all of them are upwards of 5,000 years old. I pointed this out to him.

'Honestly,' he said, still laughing. 'You've got to see it.'

I turned my attention from what I had been doing and switched on Google Earth, an excellent way of seeing just about any place on our planet from the air. It also has extremely accurate measuring facilities.

Chris gave me the coordinates and Google Earth sped across the Atlantic to Washington DC – and there it was. To the northwest of the city centre and about four miles from the Capitol, there was a structure that, from the air, looked uncannily like a British henge. Of course it wasn't one, and Chris knew it wasn't. He was already well aware that this was the US Naval Observatory, originally founded in Washington DC in 1830 and finally moved to its present home in 1893. The former governor of the Observatory had a large house on the site, now occupied by the vice president of the United States.

'Well you've got to admit it's very strange,' Chris told me. 'We know that the giant henges of Britain were observatories, and here is one in Washington DC that looks very similar.'

I agreed. 'What size is it?' I wanted to know.

'That's the interesting part,' Chris replied. 'It seems to be almost exactly 732MY in diameter.'

'No!' I exclaimed, disbelieving that such a thing would be possible.

'Measure it for yourself,' Chris responded.

That is exactly what I did, both on Google Earth and later on a large-scale map. There was no doubt about it, the US Naval Observatory Circle in Washington DC is twice 366MY and therefore 2 Megalithic Seconds of arc in diameter.

We had become well aware that the distance of 366MY, as 1 Megalithic Second of the polar Earth, should be added to Thom's measurements of the Megalithic Yard, the Megalithic Rod and the Megalithic Inch.

Of course, as we say in Britain, 'One swallow doesn't make a summer'. This could be a random chance event, so we both turned our attention to Washington DC itself. It's hard to explain what that Monday was like. The telephone and Skype calls came thick and fast and it seemed that with every passing minute one or the other of us was finding something else of significance.

The first realization that we were definitely onto something came when I looked at the area immediately to the south of the White House. Just north of the Mall, between it and the president's house, is a park known as Ellipse Park. I am now quite familiar with it, but I wasn't at the time. If you were to go there now you would find a wide expanse of open grass, where events are held, children play and people jog and walk their dogs. It didn't take me long to realize that this oval park, from the middle of the outer pedestrian path in each case and across its widest point, is 366MY, or 1 Megalithic Second of arc in diameter.

We spent all day measuring, and the next day, and the next. We obtained the best maps we could and checked to make sure Google Earth wasn't inaccurate in some way, but there was no doubt about it. There were not just one or two measurements within Washington DC that were definable as units of 366MY, there were many.

Washington DC is a city of *circles*, where small parks and traffic islands stand at the intersection of busy roads. Most of these, though often renamed these days, have been there since L'Enfant's original drawings of the proposed city were completed. Many of these were involved in what we ultimately discovered.

It soon became obvious that the main focus of the Megalithic measurements in Washington DC was at the centre of Ellipse Park. Why this should be the case we had no idea, but we feverishly continued the measuring and checking until we had explored every possibility.

The distance between the centre of the Ellipse and a point under the dome of the Capitol is 2,429 metres (7,979ft) which is 8×366MY, whilst the distance between the centre of the Ellipse and the statue at the centre of Lafayette Park, just north of the White House, is 607 metres (1,992ft), which is 2×366MY.

Lafayette Park is itself something of a node, because the distance between its centre and the centre of Mount Vernon Square, to the northeast, is 1,214 metres (3,983ft), which is 4×366MY, while being the same distance from Washington Circle to the northwest.

Back at the centre of the Ellipse we discovered that it is close to 1,822 metres from the centre of Dupont Circle to the northwest, and the same distance from Logan Circus in the northeast. Both these distances have well over a 99 per cent accuracy of measuring 6×366MY.

Over to the east we find another set of correspondences between the Capitol, Stanton Square, Steward Square and Lincoln Park, all with multiples of 366MY measurements, and forming a diamond.

We took our measurements very carefully, both on Google Earth and on maps, and although it is impossible in some cases to achieve a higher degree of accuracy than 99 per cent, with so many of the same sort of mirror-image situations emerging, there is always at least one of the mirror measurements that is virtually spot on. We have to remember that the surveying for this part of Washington was undertaken at the end of the 18th century, when measuring techniques were not what they are these days. However, what we found on the first day, together with what came later, convinces us that these were intended to be units of Megalithic measure. When they are plotted on the map something remarkable takes place.

Plotting all the Megalithic measurements in colour on a map, something neither of us expected suddenly made itself apparent. There, right in the middle of Washington DC, was a large and complex arrow, running from north to south and pointing straight to the heart of Ellipse Park!

Before I go on to explain what we discovered about Ellipse Park, and especially the centre of it, it is worth addressing an issue that occurred to us quite early in these discoveries. Why is the White House not involved in these Megalithic measures? The Capitol is certainly a major focus and, as we shall presently see, so are some of the other most famous structures in Washington DC, but it appears as though the White House itself was overlooked.

Strictly speaking this isn't the case. If we look again at Pierre Charles L'Enfant's original plan for Washington DC we can recall that it was based upon a right-angled triangle. This ran due west from the Capitol to the Jefferson Pier or Stone (where the Washington Monument was meant to be),

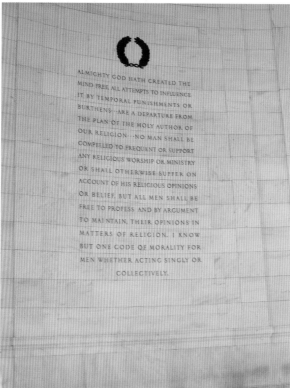

1: (Previous page) The Washington Monument; phallic expression of both God and Goddess. Picture taken from the Jefferson Memorial and on the north–south line originally intended to be the United States prime meridian.

2: A view from the middle of the Lincoln Memorial on the Mall, showing that the centre line of the Mall does not line up with the dome of the Capitol.

3: One of the speeches carved into the wall of the Jefferson Memorial showing exactly how Thomas Jefferson felt about the association of religion and state.

ALMIGHTY GOD HATH CREATED THE MIND FREE ALL ATTEMPTS TO INFLUENCE IT BY TEMPORAL PUNISHMENTS OR BURTHENS···ARE A DEPARTURE FROM THE PLAN OF THE HOLY AUTHOR OF OUR RELIGION···NO MAN SHALL BE COMPELLED TO FREQUENT OR SUPPORT ANY RELIGIOUS WORSHIP OR MINISTRY OR SHALL OTHERWISE SUFFER ON ACCOUNT OF HIS RELIGIOUS OPINIONS OR BELIEF, BUT ALL MEN SHALL BE FREE TO PROFESS AND BY ARGUMENT TO MAINTAIN, THEIR OPINIONS IN MATTERS OF RELIGION. I KNOW BUT ONE CODE OF MORALITY FOR MEN WHETHER ACTING SINGLY OR COLLECTIVELY.

4–8: Some of the many goddesses to be seen on statues and monuments around Washington DC.

9: It doesn't look much but this is the exact spot that marks the very centre of Washington DC Ellipse Park, with the small marker stone below the turf and the entrance to the subterranean vault.

10: The United States distance marker stone, showing the place from which all distances in the United States were intended to be taken, but also marking the original prime meridian of Washington DC.

11: The security helicopter that remained overhead for the whole time we were examining the centre of Ellipse Park.

12: The centre of Ellipse Park looking south along the prime meridian towards the Jefferson Memorial.

13: A view down Pennsylvania Avenue towards the Capitol – the hypotenuse of the original triangle upon which Washington DC was constructed.

14: Part of the World War II Memorial on the Mall, the latest of the constructs to show a definite Megalithic positioning within Washington DC.

15: The White House north front, looking south from Lafayette Square down the old prime meridian.

16: Lafayette Square, immediately to the north of the White House – a significant Megalithic hub.

17: Left to right, Christopher Knight and Alan Butler in Ellipse Park, Washington DC. (Picture courtesy of Christopher Knight)

18: The easternmost marker stone for the District of Columbia, put in place at the very start of the planning of Washington DC. (Picture courtesy of Christopher Knight)

19: The Capitol, Washington DC, surmounted by the Goddess of Freedom. (Picture courtesy of Christopher Knight)

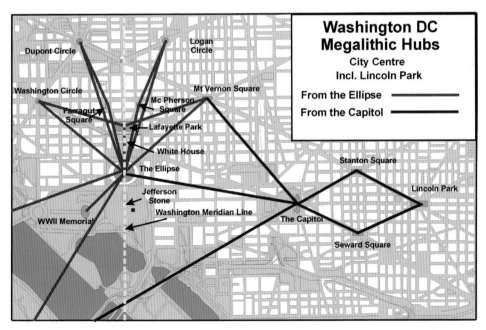

20: A map of the streets of central Washington DC including the Megalithic connections between squares and intersections.

21: The Pentagon – the most significant building in Washington DC in terms of its Megalithic credentials.

22: Masonic symbols placed by architect John Wood on the buildings in Kings Circus, Bath, England.

23: The meridian marker stone set in the ground, just below the turf at the very centre of Ellipse Park in Washington DC. Is this the entry point to the chamber below? This location is presently fenced off and out of bounds to visitors.

then turned north to the White House, before travelling southeast down what would become Pennsylvania Avenue, and to the Capitol again.

If we measure this triangle carefully we discover that the distance around its three sides is 5,771 metres (18,934ft). In Megalithic terms this is 19×366MY. In other words, the distance around L'Enfant's original right-angled triangle, upon which Washington DC was based, is equal to 19 Megalithic Seconds of arc of the Earth's polar circumference. This measurement is not an approximation – it is as near to exact as makes no difference.

We know that L'Enfant considered the intended president's house to be extremely important and, in his conception, it was to be a veritable palace. It is not surprising therefore that he made it part of his original planning. In addition, it lies on the midsummer sunset line when viewed from the Capitol,

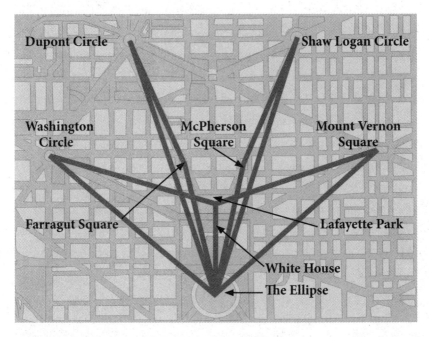

Figure 25. The Megalithic arrow in Washington DC, pointing to the centre of Ellipse Park

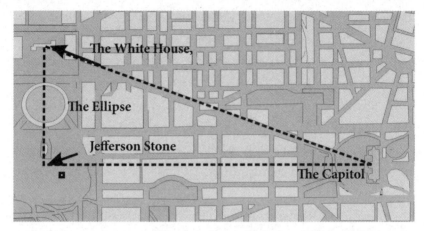

Figure 26. The original right-angled triangle upon which Washington DC was based by Pierre Charles L'Enfant. It measures 19×366 MY.

but it would also seem that L'Enfant was in possession of the Megalithic measuring system, or else had been instructed with regard to the size of this first right-angled triangle around and within which everything else would stand. That it should be such an accurate Megalithic construct *by chance* seems patently absurd, especially when all the other Megalithic measures in Washington DC are taken into account.

However, the existence of the arrow and so many Megalithic measures radiating from the centre of the Ellipse seemed especially surprising. Of course we wanted to know as much about this area of parkland as we could ascertain. In the very earliest maps for the projected new city of Washington DC there is a circle shown below the White House but, because of the scale and the lack of labelling, it is impossible to work out what this is intended to be. Later maps simply show a vacant lot to the south of the White House gardens and this seems to be exactly what Ellipse Park was for quite some time. If referred to at all, this area of land was known as the 'White Lot', apparently not in connection with the White House but because it was surrounded by a high, white fence.

We do know that Union soldiers were camped on the White Lot during the American Civil War and that they paraded there. By the time the war was over, the centre of Washington DC, and especially the area around the Mall, looked shabby. Presumably, because the standing army was still so large, it was decided to employ some of the soldiers to clean up the city. One of the jobs they undertook was the grading of the land that had formerly been the White Lot and the creation there of an ellipse-shaped park.

The man given responsibility for this job was an engineering officer by the name of Lieutenant Colonel Thomas Lincoln Casey. The work was done between 1877 and 1880 and, while it was being undertaken, Casey filed yearly reports about progress. In his 1878 report he indicated that grading for the Ellipse was proceeding well, but he noted that the exception was an area right at the centre of the Ellipse, which was inaccessible to him. Casey suggested that sewer work was taking place there, which indicates that a hole or holes were being dug. Unfortunately he was no more explicit, except to say that the work at the centre of the Ellipse was under the jurisdiction of the 'District Commissioners'.

The Ellipse eventually became part of what is known as President's Park and was ultimately the scene for all manner of functions and public events. The Ellipse has a particular significance in that it stands extremely close to the very centre of the District of Columbia. The District of Columbia, as we have seen, was originally a square of land, though diamond-shaped when seen on a map because its corners face the cardinal points. A theoretical line running for a while from the northern corner to the southern corner assumed a particular significance.

During the presidency of Thomas Jefferson, between March 1801 and March 1809, it was decided that the United States should have its own prime meridian. A prime meridian is a line of longitude from which all other lines of longitude are measured. Up to this time the United States had used the prime meridian laid down by Britain, which runs through

Greenwich, London. Thomas Jefferson personally surveyed the intended line, which ran through the middle of the White House and extended south, through what is now the Jefferson Monument on the south side of the Potomac. It is almost certain that Jefferson genuinely believed this line marked the very east–west centre of the District of Columbia diamond, but this is not actually the case.

The true north–south line connecting the northern and southern points of the Columbia diamond runs slightly to the west of the Ellipse, through a row of large properties on 17th Street. This real line of longitude dissecting the Columbia diamond runs about 296 metres (972ft) to the west of the line Jefferson laid out as being the prime meridian of the United States. The meridian marker stone went missing at some stage, but the prime meridian is marked by a relatively modern stone just north of Ellipse Park. This stone not only marks the prime meridian but also the central point from which all distances on highways across the United States were to be based.

Figure 27. The central marker stone from which all measurements across the United States were to be taken. This point stands on the intended Prime Meridian of the United States.

If I now show the same diagram, with the centre line of Columbia taken from the east and west, we can see where the centre of the District of Columbia actually is. It is not the centre of Ellipse Park but slightly to the west of it, marked by the dotted line (*see* Figures 28 & 29 overleaf).

The total discrepancy is about 330 metres (1,106ft). Jefferson was a competent surveyor and may well have realized that the line running north–south through the White House was not the *true* centre line of Columbia, but he clearly wanted the prime meridian to run through the White House and down across the vacant lot to the south of it (where the Ellipse would eventually be). The mistake may have been in the original surveying of the district, but it is much more likely to have come about because the distance between the Capitol and the White House was crucial in L'Enfant's plan and the Capitol had to be placed on top of the available hill that L'Enfant had called 'a pediment waiting for a monument'.

(If L'Enfant had placed the Capitol on what is now Capitol Hill, and then the White House on the true north–south line running through the District of Columbia, the finished right-angled triangle upon which Washington DC was placed could not have had Megalithic proportions. Also, the intended angle of the hypotenuse of the triangle, defining midsummer sunrise, would have been too shallow.)

As it turned out, the idea of a prime meridian for the United States was eventually dropped and the US ultimately reverted to using Greenwich. Nevertheless, it seems certain that the *ritual*, if not the actual centre of the District of Columbia and therefore of Washington DC, was fully intended to be located at a point in the very centre of Ellipse Park. This was exactly the spot that Lieutenant Colonel Thomas Lincoln Casey was not allowed to dig in 1878 because 'someone else' was digging there already.

Because so many of the intersections and circles in Washington DC have Megalithic relationships with the centre of the Ellipse and, bearing in mind that most of these were part of the original plan of Washington DC,

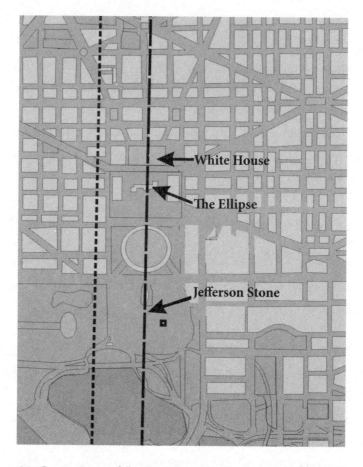

Figure 28. Centre Line of the District of Columbia north to south. The line assumed to be correct by Thomas Jefferson is on the right, whereas the true line is on the left.

it seems prudent to suggest that the Megalithic underpinning of the city was intended from the time the plans were laid. Pierre Charles L'Enfant knew about the Megalithic system, or else had been instructed concerning the dimensions he was expected to use, and it is also implied that the area that became the Ellipse had been set aside for 'something special' from the moment the city was first committed to paper.

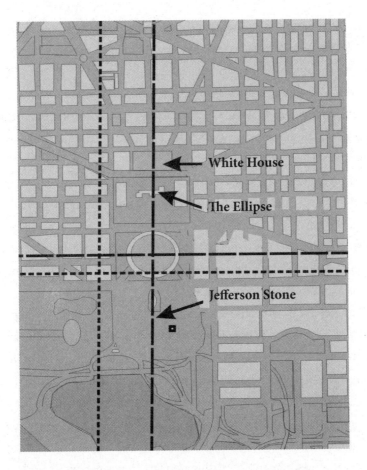

Figure 29. Presumed and actual centre lines of the District of Columbia. The long dotted lines represent the theoretical centre and the short dotted lines represent the actual centre.

If this were a crime scene, my chief suspect, for all sorts of reasons, would have to be Thomas Jefferson, and we will deal specifically with him presently. But we can't rule out George Washington either, since a capital city astride the borders of Maryland and his own native Virginia seems to have been as much his idea as anyone's.

During a recent visit to Washington DC we decided to set out to find some of the boundary stones that had been put in place when the District of Columbia was first surveyed. Many of them still remain and we took a trip to the stone that marks the easternmost boundary or 'point' of the diamond. We found it during a thunderstorm, in a small wood opposite some fairly modern houses. We were able to plot its position and that of some of its companions very carefully, using satellite navigation, and we came up with something of a surprise.

The original instructions passed by Congress for the laying out of the new district was that it should not exceed 10 miles square, by which they meant none of its sides should exceed 10 miles. A very careful measurement of the remaining stones, especially the cornerstones, reveals an interesting fact. The length of each side of the Columbia diamond is a very accurate 10 miles, but it is also something else.

Ten miles (16,098 metres) is also 53×366MY, to a high degree of accuracy. This is one of very few meeting points of the Megalithic system and the statute system of measurement and, once again, it has to be said that if this is nothing more than a coincidence, it is a very strange one. A much more likely scenario is that someone knew about the coincidence of the two systems at this point and hit upon the 10 mile square as a result.

Before we move on or come any further up to date concerning the Megalithic measurements of Washington DC, the reader has a right to know if I have the slightest proof that any of the originators of the free United States or Washington DC left any evidence that they might somehow have been party to a measuring system that, as far as we can tell, apart from Bath, had not been used for nearly 4,000 years. In fact I do have such proof, which is both intriguing and very enlightening. It brings us back, once again, to that most enigmatic character, Thomas Jefferson.

CHAPTER NINE

A MAN FOR ALL SEASONS

Thomas Jefferson and Measuring Systems

Thomas Jefferson was not only a peerless statesman, the third president of a free United States and the writer of the American Declaration of Independence; he was also one of the most remarkable men to grace the late 18th and early 19th century. Rather than to note all his interests it would be quicker and easier to make a list of what didn't fascinate Jefferson at some stage in his life. He was, amongst other things, a lawyer, political thinker, diplomat, moral philosopher, scientist, farmer, engineer, talented writer and a fierce opponent of state-sponsored religion.

In the field of science alone he could have chosen a career from at least half a dozen different disciplines; he was fascinated by astronomy, good at surveying, adept with practical inventions, an amateur doctor and a tireless and constant meteorologist. Jefferson set standards in archaeology that would not be paralleled or bettered for over a century and he excelled at palaeontology, botany and horology. His mind was never still and his curiosity was boundless. He left a legacy to a world that would have been somewhat impoverished without his presence and he truly deserves the epithet 'a man for all seasons'.

Thomas Jefferson was born in April 1743, into an influential Virginian family. His father was a surveyor, a skill that he readily taught his son, though Thomas chose law for a career, whilst at the same time never forgetting the practical grounding he had received.

At school Thomas was diligent and fascinated by everything. Because he came from a wealthy family he received the best tuition available but he was especially lucky to have been taught by Professor William Small at the College of William and Mary at Williamsburg. The young Jefferson got on well with the affable and brilliant Small, who introduced him to the work of the writers, thinkers and scientists John Locke, Francis Bacon and Isaac Newton, whom Jefferson later referred to as 'The three greatest men the world has ever produced'.

Jefferson's father, Peter, died when Thomas was only 14 and, being the eldest son, he came into the family estates, which totalled some 5,000 acres of very productive land. Thomas also acquired dozens of slaves, though there was nothing remotely odd about this in the context of his station and where he was living.

In later years Jefferson seemed to have suffered repeated and prolonged pangs of conscience about the issue of slavery. He claimed: 'We have the wolf by the ears and we can neither safely hold him, nor let him go.' By this he meant that he understood that slavery was an abomination in a moral sense, but it was considered that many landowning families in his part of America would probably lose their land and their economic base if slavery were abolished. Jefferson cannot be considered an abolitionist but he treated his slaves well, educated many and was also happy in 1778 to be involved with passing legislation to stop the importation of new slaves into the area. He said of the bill: 'It stopped the increase of the evil by importation, leaving to future efforts its final eradication.'

Jefferson's chief problem with his natural leanings to end slavery was financial. Throughout much of his life he was in debt and his slaves were part of the collateral that allowed him to borrow money to keep his estate running. To remain solvent he had to hold onto them, despite the fact that practically every sinew in his body must have told him that the whole business was disgusting.

After college Jefferson decided on a career in law. It was hard going at first, but he eventually showed just how much energy and tenacity he possessed. He was soon representing some of the most powerful and influential people in Virginia and gained a reputation for being astute and able.

In between travelling to pursue his career, Jefferson embarked on one of his lifelong passions – the creation of one of the most beautiful but modest houses ever to be built in Virginia. He called it Monticello. It was a neo-classical house, custom-built to cope with Jefferson's wide-ranging interests and a place in which he could bring up a family. The house still exists and is considered one of the United States' most treasured possessions.

It was a natural adjunct to his legal career for Thomas to become involved in politics, and he had a natural inclination for it. He represented Albemarle County in the Virginia House of Burgesses, starting in 1796. As feelings between the colonies and Great Britain started to heat up, Thomas soon made his own opinions felt. He published a pamphlet entitled 'A Summary View of the Rights of British America' and, by so doing, he fell straight under the radar of the British authorities. This little pamphlet acted as a stimulus to what eventually became open rebellion, and it became part of the framework of the later Declaration of Independence.

When the Second Continental Congress was convened in 1775, Jefferson was one of the delegates. He was a keen advocate of independence and was chosen as one of five members who were to draft a declaration. Probably because he was a noted writer, he was chosen to write the Declaration of Independence and, although he was only one of five people involved, it is clear from his later writings that the words framing the Declaration of Independence were his.

Jefferson was a declared traitor and, if the British authorities had ever laid hands on him, his life would have been worth nothing. Undaunted, he continued his political career in Virginia and in 1781 came within a few minutes of being captured by a British raiding party during the War of Independence.

In June 1783 Virginia sent Jefferson to the Congress of Confederation, where he approached Congress with a proposal relating to measurements and money. By 1785 he had been chosen to represent the new United States in France, and so he set off across the Atlantic. He peerlessly served the States in France for five years, though he was probably not too happy amidst French society and was glad to come home and to take up the post of Secretary of State under George Washington.

At the end of 1793 Thomas took a break from political life and spent some time at his beloved Monticello. But it wasn't too long before he was back in harness again and in 1796 he ran for the presidency. In the end he lost out to John Adams but he was made vice president. Finally, in February of 1801 he became the third president of the United States, a position he would hold for eight years.

After a sometimes rough ride in the White House, Jefferson was glad enough to return to Virginia, but he remained as active as ever and was able to help found the University of Virginia, which had been one of his longstanding dreams.

In temperament, Thomas Jefferson was moderate and not given to anger or fits of pique. He respected his political opponents but would always fight fiercely for something in which he really believed. His policies as president were generally sensible and, like George Washington, he would avoid doing anything that threatened the stability of the new nation or undermined its positive influence abroad.

Despite views on slavery that were somewhat forced on him by the age and by circumstance, Jefferson genuinely did believe in the three virtues of Liberty, Equality and Brotherhood. Jefferson appeared to be the perfect Freemason, though there is not the slightest evidence that he ever was one. However, 'Every Jesuit is a Catholic but not every Catholic is a Jesuit'.

When it came to religion it is often suggested that Jefferson never took a stand, except to be quite adamant that Church and State should not mix. He was fiercely opposed to any nation having a particular religion forced upon it by law or even encouraged by government. He said that if someone living next door to him had 10 gods, it should not take a penny from his pocket.

Avery Dulles (1918–2008), a leading Catholic priest, cardinal and noted theologian, probably summed up Thomas Jefferson's religion the best, at least in its public setting:

> In summary, then, Jefferson was a Deist because he believed in one God, in divine Providence, in the divine moral Law, and in rewards and punishments after death; but he did not believe in supernatural revelation. He was a Christian Deist because he saw Christianity as the highest expression of natural religion and Jesus as an incomparably great moral teacher. He was not an orthodox Christian because he rejected, among other things, the doctrines that Jesus was the promised Messiah and the incarnate Son of God. Jefferson's religion is fairly typical of the American form of Deism in his day.

Deism is a belief in God, but not one tied to a specific creed. In fact Jefferson admired Jesus greatly, though merely as a moral guide. He believed that all the miracles spoken about in the New Testament were added after the event, and for effect. Nevertheless he often stated that he thought the teachings of Jesus represented the best moral standpoint ever expressed. As president he attended church services – probably because it was expedient to do so – but he never took Holy Communion. In his religious beliefs Thomas

Jefferson comes across as an archetypal Freemason, or at least someone supremely fitted for the role, though once again there is no evidence that he embraced the Craft.

This is not the first time I have researched the life of Thomas Jefferson. He became important to Chris Knight and myself when we were researching our book *Civilization One*, because on 13 July 1790 Jefferson put a report to the House of Representatives called 'Plan for Establishing Uniformity in the Coinage, Weights and Measures of the United States'.

Some background is in order here. That august body, the Royal Society, had been established in London in November 1660, when 12 men interested in the promotion and study of science got together at Gresham College in London. However, this meeting was not the first of its sort. Even during the reign of Queen Elizabeth I, which ended in 1603, people of a scientific bent were getting together, somewhat clandestinely, in a group that gradually became known as the 'Invisible College'.

They had to be careful because England was in a religious ferment and nobody knew if the repressive aspects of the Catholic Church would once again come to dominate the country. It wasn't until the beginning of the reign of Charles II that a sense of greater security was brought to bear on religion (though even then it didn't last). However, with the restoration of Charles II in 1661, after the English Civil War and over a decade of kingless rule in England, these early scientists felt safe enough to make known both themselves and their common efforts to promote science.

They talked about all manner of things, and they were allowed to do so partly because Charles II approved of their endeavours and sought their expertise in the creation of the powerful navy that Britain so badly needed. One of their points of discussion was an effort to standardize weights and measures, not just in Britain but also across the entire globe.

This was not an effort that sat in isolation. There was a firm belief that humanity had lost something of tremendous importance. It was felt that our species had once shared a common language and a common way of looking at matters such as weights and measures. People pointed to Old Testament stories such as that of the Tower of Babel, which explicitly stated that there had once been a common tongue and a shared heritage. Even extremely intelligent thinkers of the age thought that this commonality could be re-established. This notion is important and stands at the heart of many of my observations in this book.

One man took the bull by the horns and set out to re-establish not only the lost common language of humanity, but also to suggest a new way of creating weights and measures that could be accepted by everyone – thus fostering foreign trade, upon which nations such as Britain relied heavily.

The man in question was John Wilkins, an English clergyman, supporter of the Parliamentarian cause in the English Civil War, and a freethinker with whom Thomas Jefferson would have had much in common. Wilkins was born in 1614 and ordained around 1637 and, although he was an avid supporter of the Church of England and was for four years the Bishop of Chester, he was a fair-dealing, open-minded individual who believed that the divisions within Protestantism during his era could be sorted out, with inclusion into the Church of England for at least some Nonconformists.

Wilkins was one of the founder members of the Royal Society. He was on good terms with people in and around London who would become household names, such as Robert Hooke, William Petty and Robert Boyle. Wilkins also knew Sir Christopher Wren and was himself something of a polymath, even though his name has more or less been forgotten in the annals of early science.

Even Wilkins' ideas on the reforming of weights and measures were not new. Some of them came from Simon Stevin (1547–1620). Stevin was a Flemish-born early scientist and inventor. He first put forward the notion that the lost age of wisdom could be recovered, if only we were all able to speak the original language (which for some reason he thought might have been akin to Dutch). Stevin made an attempt at new weights and measures, though not in any depth, but he did promote the idea that a fully decimal system might be employed.

Wilkins was doubtless aware of Simon Stevin's work, but he went much further in his suggestions for weights and measures. He was probably the first individual in relatively modern times to suggest that all measurements should originate from a pendulum capable of beating once during 1 second of time. Since Wilkins was well aware that if experiments with pendulums were always carried out at the same latitude and the same altitude, the result would always be the same, he saw the use of the seconds pendulum as being a reliable way of formulating a new measuring system. At the same time he advocated the possibility of using a division of the Earth's circumference to establish his basic linear length, an idea that predated the French, who at the end of the 18th century created the metric system.

A French near-contemporary of Wilkins, the astronomer Jean Picard (1620–82), may have taken up Wilkins' ideas and run with them, because he espoused an almost identical system. There is no proof that Picard knew of Wilkins' work and it is quite possible that he had reached the same conclusions in isolation.

All the same, there is so much about the metric system that came into use in France at the end of the 18th century that smacks of the tireless work of John Wilkins. We can hardly doubt that there is some sort of connection – and that connection is likely to have been Thomas Jefferson, who was in France for four years, between 1785 and 1789. During that time he would have been rubbing shoulders with many of the men involved in the French Academy of Sciences. Initially Jefferson, together with the older John Adams and the much older Benjamin Franklin, was kept busy organizing treaties and trade deals for the United States with a number of European states but, for most of his time in France, Thomas had little to do except represent the United States socially (which he almost certainly did not enjoy).

He was based in a classy mansion in the middle of Paris, giving him a chance to mix with some of France's brightest and best intellectuals. Since Jefferson was almost obsessed with scientific advancement, he would have been involved with members of the French Academy of Sciences. It was here that he doubtless discussed the intended metric system of weights and measures with the French scientists. (An explanation of the metric system and the much more ancient Sumerian system of weights and measures can be found in Appendix Two).

During his tenure in Paris Jefferson travelled to London to spend some months in England, when he travelled around a great deal, mainly looking at some of England's newest and grandest mansions. It is entirely possible, in fact more than likely, that he visited the city of Bath, which was all the rage at the time and was considered the cutting edge of English neoclassicism and sophistication. If so, he would certainly have seen John Wood's King's Circus. One of the main reasons for Jefferson's protracted stay in England and the journeys he made was to see the latest versions of the classical architecture that he loved so much. He also visited the south of France and Italy for the same reason and as a result there can be little doubt that his influence would have a great bearing on the designs that would be adopted for Washington DC.

As far as the metric system of measurement is concerned, the final plan adopted by the French is virtually a carbon copy of the ideas of John Wilkins, and these ideas could easily have reached the ears of influential members of the French Academy of Sciences via Thomas Jefferson. The speed with which Jefferson put together his own considerations regarding a new measuring system when he got back to America demonstrates that it had been on his mind for some time because his system could not have been worked out in even a few months. It is plainly a study that took years. It is true that Jefferson was asked to submit a report on the matter, but this was probably because he had requested to be asked.

Jefferson began his report on weights and measures by explaining the background. He suggested that he had been interested in such matters for a long time and spoke in detail about some of his observations regarding apparently diverse measuring systems, showing that in reality there was no diversity at all and that many of them were clearly just modifications of a lost, earlier system.

This is one of the facts regarding Jefferson's report that immediately attracted our attention. Chris and I had come to realize that many units of measurement still in use in the United States today (and still used regularly in Britain) originate from the Megalithic Yard. This is true of the Imperial pint, in terms of liquid measure, and the statute pound in terms of weight. In the case of liquid, the pint was derived from creating a cube with sides of $\frac{1}{10}$th of a Megalithic Yard and then filling such a vessel with water. The result is a modern pint.

We also discovered that dry weights, such as the pound (lb), were derived from using the same $\frac{1}{10}$th MY cube and filling it with cereal grain. Strangely, it does not matter w at grain is used, since wheat, barley, oats or even un-hulled rice all do the same job. The weight of such grain comes out as being the same as a modern pound.

It is hard to believe that the relatively modern pound and pint could have originated in a measuring system that ostensibly disappeared 4,000 years ago. Indeed, we have had little success in persuading scientists that this was the case. It isn't that they disagree, more that they refuse to even look at our figures because the whole scenario seems so unlikely; but, we don't invent this evidence, we merely report it. It is not simply the pound and pint that relate to the Megalithic system, but practically every weight and measure in the Imperial system, because they are all linked one to another. It has always seemed to me that the reason experts won't look at our evidence in a public sense is *because* it is so irrefutable. Even scientists do not like to be confronted with information they cannot rationally explain. It is better to keep quiet and maintain the status quo.

After explaining the background to all the measuring systems he had studied, Jefferson went on to suggest that the means of establishing the start of any rational measuring system were limited. He said there was nothing in the natural world of an irrefutable and unchanging size upon which a unit of length could be based and, as we had done when looking at the Megalithic system, he suggested that the only means of creating such a unit was by recourse to the turning Earth itself.

As the Earth turns on its axis it does so at a rate that is so fixed that, for all reasonable purposes, it never changes. If that fact could be harnessed and turned into a known and constant linear unit, it could be recaptured at any time. Like us, Jefferson opted for the length of a pendulum. In the Megalithic system the length of the pendulum had been set by recourse to the movements of the planet Venus – but this was merely the 'clock' against which the swings of the pendulum were counted.

By Jefferson's time there were some very accurate clocks about. John Harrison (1693–1776) had created a sequence of ever more accurate marine chronometers, mostly for the purpose of making navigation easier at sea, but by Jefferson's time such accurate timepieces were finding their way around the world. Indeed, Jefferson had one himself, which he had commissioned locally.

Jefferson was in favour of the seconds pendulum, which had previously been suggested by John Wilkins and the French Jean Picard, and the length of which had been defined accurately by Isaac Newton. But it was at this point that Jefferson deviated from earlier ideas and it is fair to say that, during our research for *Civilization One*, Chris and I did not entirely understand why he had done so.

The seconds pendulum (a pendulum that would swing from left to right or right to left in 1 second of time), when measured from the point of suspension to the centre of the weight and checked at 45° latitude, according to Isaac Newton would measure 39.14912in (99.438764cm), but Jefferson was not content with this. He maintained that there was some difficulty regarding the swing of the pendulum (though no other contemporary researcher had mentioned it) and said he preferred to use a 'rod' rather than a free-swinging pendulum.

He suggested, quite rightly, that if a very fine rod were used instead of a string with a weight on the end, it would have to be half as long again than such a string and weight, in order to achieve the same objective. This meant that a seconds rod that would swing once back and forth in exactly 1 second would measure 58.72368in (149.158147cm). This was the unit he proposed to base his entire system upon, by dividing into five equal parts and by calling each part 1 foot. The actual length of the Jefferson foot would therefore have been 11.744736in (29.83162944cm).

Jefferson then proposed to use this basic unit to devise all units of length, volume and mass, by using increments of tens, hundreds and thousands. So, ten Jefferson feet would equal a Jefferson decad, ten Jefferson decads would equal one Jefferson rood, ten Jefferson roods would equal one Jefferson furlong and ten Jefferson furlongs would equal one Jefferson mile.

The Jefferson foot would be divided into ten Jefferson inches, the inch divided into ten Jefferson lines and each Jefferson line divided into ten Jefferson points.

Jefferson's measure of capacity would be based on a cubic Jefferson foot, and for weights Thomas envisaged a cubic Jefferson inch of rainwater as the primary measurement of weight, which he called a Jefferson ounce.

There were divisions and subdivisions at every stage and in each category of weights and measures, but the tens, hundreds and thousands were present in each case.

This method is very close to the metric system, except for the initial unit of linear length. In the metric system, the basic unit was the metre, which was taken as being 1×10,000,000th part of a quadrant of the Earth stretching from the North Pole to the Equator. As such, it was not exactly the same length as Jefferson's basic unit or indeed the seconds pendulum defined with a string and a weight. The seconds pendulum would measure 39.14912in (99.438764cm), whereas the proposed French metre was very slightly longer at 39.37007874in (100cm). In other words the French system was based upon the size of the Earth, which Jefferson considered to be unreliable and difficult to know for certain. (The French did, however, suggest that if the metre was lost it could be found again by recourse to the seconds pendulum.)

By opting for a rod instead of a pendulum, Thomas Jefferson changed the ground rules in a way no other commentator on standardizing measurements had done.

It did not take us long to realize that there were a number of direct correlations between Jefferson's proposed system of the measurements and the Megalithic system. For example, although Jefferson had not opted for a geodetic measuring unit (one that divides equally and logically the circumference of the Earth), he achieved exactly that when one bears in mind the Megalithic form of geometry. What is more, it achieves this objective in numbers that are tied directly to the Megalithic system and which are far from random.

What we found is this: Jefferson proposed that there were to be 1,000 Jefferson feet to a Jefferson furlong, but we discovered that 366 Jefferson furlongs are the same as 1 Megalithic degree of arc of the Earth's polar circumference, to a very high degree of accuracy:

366 Jefferson furlongs = 109.1837km (67.8437 miles)

1 Megalithic degree of polar Earth = 109.3167km (67.9262 miles)

We had no real idea how this could have come about, but the implications went further. Because there are 366 Megalithic degrees to the circumference of the Earth, it stands to reason that there are 366×366 Jefferson furlongs to the polar circumference of the Earth. The accuracy is stunning and easily beats 99.5 per cent. In effect, the Megalithic Yard that hides within Jefferson's system is only 1mm shorter than the Megalithic Yard suggested by the research of Alexander Thom – the unit we had been working with for so long!

We thought about the problem and were finally forced to come to the conclusion that there was something very special about the second of time and the pendulum that measures it, that automatically resonates with the Megalithic system and the pendulum upon which its primary linear length, the Megalithic Yard, is based. However, this was never possible for us to *prove* in a mathematical sense. Neither of us has ceased looking for such a provable relationship since then, but we are no closer to discovering it than we ever were. What is more, this sort of coincidence does not take place between the metric system and the Megalithic system, or with a system based on the true seconds pendulum and the Megalithic system. It is only present when the starting point is the seconds rod that Jefferson chose to use.

To put it at its simplest, there is a meeting point between Jefferson's basic unit of measurement and its multiples, and the size of the Megalithic degree of the polar Earth; 366,000 Jefferson feet is the same as 131,760 MY. What is more, Jefferson's system is geodetic, but only if viewed using Megalithic geometry.

The more one thinks about this, the more incredible it seems. As far as we were aware when we wrote *Civilization One*, Thomas Jefferson knew nothing about Megalithic geometry and nothing about Megalithic measurements – but how could such an obvious meeting of two randomly chosen systems have provided these results? It seems so far beyond chance that there must be an intention.

When we discovered how many instances of the use of the Megalithic

Yard and of Megalithic geometry there were in the creation of Washington DC, the situation changed. It is quite clear that someone who was close to the planning of the city was more than aware of Megalithic measurements and geometry, and under these circumstances it would not be at all odd to see that Thomas Jefferson, in his suggestions for a new system of weights and measures, incorporated the Megalithic system into it.

Jefferson would have known that to try to recreate the integrated Megalithic measuring system in a complete form would have been impossible. For more than 3,000 years or more the world had been committed to working within a geometric framework of 360° to a circle. To try to alter this would have meant Jefferson going so far out on a limb that fellow scientists surely would have laughed at him.

However, what Jefferson's proposed system does highlight is the existence of Megalithic geometry. What he suggested was a stroke of genius because it offered a metric system, which those of a scientific disposition had been hinting at for a couple of centuries, but at the heart of this metric system the basics of the Megalithic system remained, so that anyone with the requisite knowledge could recognize the fact. That is precisely what Chris Knight and I had done, even if at first we failed to understand what was happening.

The Megalithic Yard itself does not appear in Jefferson's system – it is *implied*. The fact that 366 Jefferson furlongs equal 1 Megalithic degree of the Earth's polar circumference is the most inspired aspect, because it retains, at the very heart of the new system, a positive clue about the old system. It also makes the system geodetic to anyone who knows about 366° geometry.

The reader must make up his or her own mind, but in my comprehension there is no coincidence here. It seems to me that Thomas Jefferson clearly knew about the Megalithic system. The implied Megalithic Yard he incorporated into his own metric system was only at odds with the real

Megalithic Yard by one millimetre, and even this may have been unavoida-ble because of the needs of providing a pendulum with a one-second swing.

Unfortunately, and for reasons we cannot fully understand, Jefferson's suggestions for a new measuring system were not adopted in the United States. There could be a number of reasons. Only a few days after Jefferson offered his report to the House of Representatives, the French Academy of Science submitted its own suggestions for a metric system. However, this cannot have been the reason why the United States rejected Jefferson's report because the United States never did take the metric system on board.

The most likely explanation for Jefferson's report being either sidelined or simply ignored is that it was too good, or rather too informative, regarding the Megalithic system. In other words, there were people present in the United States government who wanted to keep this information to themselves.

This is a pity because Jefferson's system of weights and measures was at least as good as the metric system. It was based on a one-second rod, which, if measured at the same latitude and the same altitude, would never vary. The metric system meanwhile had the distinction of being wrong from the very start. The metre was based on a polar circumference of the Earth of what we would now refer to as 40,000 kilometres and, though this is a fair approximation, it is not entirely correct.

In closing this chapter, one thought occurs to me. The United States never accepted the metric system. It retains the same units of weight and measure (with just a few modifications) that it inherited from Britain, even though Britain itself has now officially adopted the metric system. But these same units, which include the pound and the pint, owe their own origi-nation to the Megalithic system. It could be that there were those at the heart of the United States government who knew this and were reticent to abandon something so old and time-served.

Ultimately, the reason why Jefferson's ingenious system of weights and

measures was not adopted must remain within the realms of conjecture.
But one thing is certain; the evidence that someone in high authority in
the early United States fully understood the Megalithic system was now
growing so strong that it simply could not be ignored.

CHAPTER TEN

THE RISE OF
THE STAR FAMILIES

Enoch, the Shekinah and the Temple of Jerusalem

The discovery that those planning and building Washington DC were in possession of knowledge that went back thousands of years, and measuring systems that had not been used since around 2000 BC, ought to have been so surprising that we might well have dismissed it out of hand. Well we might, were it not for the fact that information coming to light regarding the foundation of Washington DC actually confirmed suspicions that both Chris Knight and I already had about the survival of truly ancient ideas and beliefs.

Coming at the situation from two different directions, Chris and I have both been convinced, from the very start of our research, that there is a common thread running through society, which has been in place for many centuries. I once referred to it as 'the golden thread through the tapestry of time'. It involves a group of people whose ideas and motivations have often been at odds with the mainstream society of their times, and yet are individuals who have always seemed able to acquire power and to manipulate events to suit their own purposes. Generally speaking these people sought peace and prosperity for a world built on common aims and objectives. They have always maintained a 'one world' view, and have envisaged a planet ruled from a single, custom-created capital. They have also exhibited religious beliefs and practices that are at odds with the norm.

A 'golden thread' is probably a good analogy because it is hard to locate these people in most periods and situations, yet when they do appear they stand out in startling isolation from the background of history. Chris first identified them as being the people who ultimately created Freemasonry, though in the *Hiram Key*, Chris and Robert Lomas push the foundation of the group that were to promote Freemasonry right back to the Near East and the originators of the Jewish people.

Meanwhile, working on *The Bronze Age Computer Disc*, I began to uncover a lost way of looking at the world, measuring every aspect of it, that seems to be spectacular, even by the standards of modern mathematics. It turned out our ideas merged in the early days of our individual research in terms of geographical location. I was dealing with the Minoans from the island of Crete, whose prehistoric culture seems to have had so much in common with the Neolithic peoples of the Mediterranean and those further west and north in Spain, France and Britain, but I finally discovered that there was a real and tangible connection between the Minoans and the pre-Jewish peoples of the Near East too.

It is now known that the Minoans, who were great seafarers and traders, had settlements along the coast and even inland in the Levant. Minoan-style pottery has been found in Gaza, and Minoan-type settlements have been located close to the Sea of Galilee and in the Jordan Valley. It is more than possible that people escaping from Crete, after the horrendous series of natural disasters following the eruption of the volcano that formed the island of Santorini around 1450 BC but possibly as far back as 1650 BC, influenced some of the civilizations that started to develop along the coast of the Near East.

About the same time as the Santorini eruption, the Egyptians began to talk about the 'Sea Peoples' – raiders of unknown origins who were causing problems for existing cultures down the Levant and into the Nile Delta. It is likely that these sea peoples were the ancestors of the Philistines, who are mentioned repeatedly in the Old Testament. With such long-term displacement caused by the Santorini event, which may well have been the greatest volcanic eruption in human experience, and with incursions into Crete of the Mycenaeans from the mainland of Greece, it would not be surprising to find aspects of Minoan culture being brought by these 'displaced pirates' and asserting a strong influence on the Near East, which is, after all, quite close to Crete.

Because of the apparent evidence offered by the Old Testament, we tend to think of the history of the region being akin to the stories left to us by just one group of people – the Hebrews. But the story of what happened in the Near East in Bronze Age and Iron Age times is far more complex and convoluted than we can learn from the Bible. We might think of the Old Testament as being more akin to propaganda than history. In addition, many of the stories of the Old Testament were written or rewritten long after the eras in which they took place, and many of them were also subject to influence from outside cultures, such as that of the Babylonians at the time that many Hebrews were held in captivity there.

Rabbinical Judaism of the kind the world knows today is a far cry from the religion of the Hebrews. The Hebrews, or Hiberu, were nomadic pastoralists who maintained their flocks and travelled around looking for grazing. It is likely that they entered the region later known as Canaan around 2000 BC or later. In the Bible we can see the Hebrews gathering together and conquering other peoples, both before and after their supposed stay in Egypt.

Chief among those mentioned as being enemies of the Hebrews were the Philistines. Old Testament accounts pour scorn on the religious practices of people such as the Philistines, but what the Bible does not tell us is just how similar the beliefs of the Hebrews might have been for much of their early history. As I have suggested, to turn the gods of one's enemies into the devils of one's own is commonplace and that is exactly what takes place time and again in the Old Testament.

Like many pastoralists the Hebrews venerated a male storm god, who with the passing of time took on the persona of the Jehovah of biblical times. But we know that at least until the advent of King Solomon (around 1000 BC) the Hebrew storm god did not reign supreme in the hearts of the Hebrews. Solomon himself is admonished in the Old Testament for 'going after Ashtoreth the goddess of the Sidonians' (1 Kings 11:5). Ashtoreth was the name used in the Old Testament to describe the Semitic Mother Goddess, who was alternatively called Astarte in Phoenicia, Ishtar in Babylonia and Athta in Arabia.

The Bible also tells us that when Solomon wanted to create a great temple in Jerusalem, he called upon Hiram the King of Tyre to design the building and create it. Ashtoreth was certainly worshipped in Tyre, which was not a Hebrew area, and so it might seem strange that Solomon should call upon what he ought to have considered non-believers to build the most important religious site in his kingdom. In reality it appears that Ashtoreth was for centuries worshipped side by side with the Hebrew Storm God. Only in later times was the Goddess dropped. To many of the Hebrews' neighbours she retained her old status alongside the Storm God, who in the Old Testament is often referred to as Baal.

It is quite likely that the rulers of Tyre were also legatees of the 'sea peoples'. They were known to be great astronomers and their culture produced wonderful craftsmen, which is precisely why Solomon chose them to build his temple.

King Solomon was particularly interested in a phenomenon known as the Shekinah. Chris and Robert Lomas dealt in length with the Shekinah in their book *Uriel's Machine*, a work for which I supplied some of the background astronomical information. The Shekinah was the coming together of the planets Mercury and Venus at dawn, on very specific dates, associated with the solstices and possibly the equinoxes. That the idea of the Shekinah and its power was a totally Hebrew concept is in some doubt.

It should be remembered that the Hebrews were an extended series of tribes of nomads. Up until the founding of Israel they were certainly not empire builders and had lived a fairly primitive and hand-to-mouth existence. It wasn't until they had conquered a significant area of the Near East that they began to coalesce into what might be termed a civilization. After having invaded the region, Solomon's father, David, re-founded the city of Jerusalem – it was already ancient when he arrived there around 1000 BC.

The Shekinah was associated with kingship in the minds of the Semitic people of the region and this had almost certainly been the case for a very long time. Chris and Robert Lomas unearthed significant evidence to show that Solomon and the people around him who consolidated the Hebrew hold on Jerusalem were avid followers of an earlier character from the history of the Semitic people. This man was Enoch, whose life and exploits were already ancient by the time the Hebrews began to forge a single identity, and also by the time they conquered Jerusalem.

According to tradition, Enoch had been a grandson of Noah, the biblical character who survived the flood and who was supposedly especially beloved of God. Enoch had been an observer and chronicler of events associated with a mysterious group known simply as 'the Watchers', who appear to have been semi-divine. Enoch wrote down everything he saw, and also listed parables and instructions from God. The whole work came together in the Book of Enoch, a fantastical work which was lost to the West for many centuries.

The Book of Enoch had been popular with the Hebrews and also with very early Christians, but it disappeared soon after the fall of the

Jerusalem Temple in AD 70. It only came back to the West thanks to the efforts of a Freemasonic Scots adventurer called James Bruce who, in 1773, returned to Britain from Ethiopia with not one but three copies of the book. Finds amongst the Dead Sea Scrolls, located in the Jordan Valley in the 1940s, included fragments of the lost Book of Enoch and these proved that the copies Bruce had located were genuine.

Enoch had travelled widely and Chris and Robert demonstrated that he had journeyed far to the west, visiting a structure that sounds uncannily like a Megalithic passage mound. His description resembles Newgrange, a chambered tomb in the Boyne Valley of Ireland. Enoch was mightily impressed, and there is such a wealth of astronomical information in the Book of Enoch that one is left in little doubt that Enoch had been carefully tutored by these 'star priests' far to the west. Chris and I showed in our book *Before the Pyramids* that the Megalithic peoples of the British Isles had been astounding astronomers, clearly with much to impart to an astonished Enoch.

The Shekinah had been important from at least Enoch's time onwards, and it was Solomon's intention in Jerusalem to create an observatory that was specifically designed to capture the light of the Shekinah and to have an Enochian priesthood onboard that could calculate the arrival of the phenomenon. The Temple of Jerusalem was particularly well suited to this purpose; it faced east and Jerusalem itself occupies a particularly significant location. This is because the extremes of the Sun's position on the eastern horizon at dawn lie at exactly 30° north and south of east at the latitude of Jerusalem. Chris has shown that the shadows cast as a result of this are what ultimately created the famous six-pointed star, now known as the Star of David.

In addition, the view from the terrace of the old Temple of Jerusalem made it an observatory par excellence, and the building was so designed that the light from the Shekinah would fall directly through a dormer and into the Holy of Holies (the place in the Temple where the Ark of the Covenant was kept). It was believed in the very early days of the Hebrew nation that the light of the Holy Shekinah prophesied the coming of a new king. It was also thought that the very light of the Shekinah making contact with the Ark of the Covenant, a wooden box originally made to contain God's Commandments, represented a coming together of the forces of the sky (the God) and the Earth (the Goddess).

The planet Venus represented the main component of the Shekinah and, even on its own, it is the brightest object in our skies apart from the Sun and the Moon. Venus is also a very obliging planet in that, when seen from Earth, it appears to go through 8-year and 40-year cycles. This is because the orbit of the Earth around the Sun and that of Venus are synchronous. The orbital period of Venus when seen from the Earth, right around the heavens and back to its starting point is 584 days. Five such periods is almost exactly equal to eight Earth years. This effectively means that, when viewed from the surface of the Earth, Venus will always be back in the same part of space at the same time of the year after 40 Earth years.

Herein lies one of the early connections between the research Chris was undertaking and my own efforts. I knew that the number patterns on the Phaistos Disc indicated a calendar round with a duration of 40 years and, as such, it seemed to me to be a safe bet that there was a Venus component involved in the calendar. I went on to discover that the Phaistos Disc, in addition to offering an extremely efficient rectification process for the Earth year, was also a device for tracking not only Venus but also the planet Mercury. The Phaistos Disc also offers continuity, in that it would be possible to utilize it for much more than one 40-year period. It simply goes round and round, and supplies any necessary corrections that need to be made in order to track Venus and Mercury extremely accurately. It would therefore be ideally suited to tracking the occurrence of the Shekinah.

The convergence of Mercury and Venus is a fairly common happening but on most occasions when the two planets are close together in the sky they are only *relatively* close. There is a gap between them in a north–south sense (called zodiacal latitude) and they can easily be distinguished as two separate bodies. Only much more rarely do they come so close that the combined light of the two planets appears to converge, and this event is even rarer when one wishes to track it at a particular point of the year – for example at a solstice or an equinox.

In biblical times, to observe a Shekinah at the winter solstice and then to see another Shekinah in exactly the same place, would have taken 3×480 years – 1,440 years. This was considered the most mystical and powerful of any Shekinah, heralding a new epoch and not merely the time for a new king.

There was a Shekinah of this sort due around the year AD 1, and this was a time when the Jews were definitely expecting a Messiah to show up. In fact the 'star in the east' mentioned in the New Testament in association with the birth of Jesus is almost certain to be the Shekinah. The region was filled with unrest at the time because everyone knew that with the Shekinah would come a redeeming Messiah, who would defeat the enemies of Israel, most notably the Romans, and herald a wonderful new age.

We know from our combined past research that Jerusalem was the home of the group of Enochian priests set up by Solomon when the Temple was built. It is a fair bet that these priests were competent astronomers. It is also more than likely that Minoan influence, at least in terms of astronomy and mathematics, was involved in the computations made at the Temple. The influence of the Sea People along the shores of the Levant during this period is undoubted.

By the time King Hiram of Tyre was called upon by Solomon to build his new Temple, the remnants of the Cretans who had escaped the island four centuries earlier would already have been subsumed into the local populations of the Levant. We know for sure that this must have been the case because, at a time contemporary with the after-effects of the Santorini eruption (circa 1200 BC), the then King of Tyre appealed to the Egyptians because his state was being attacked. No help was forthcoming and Tyre fell prey to the Sea People. Evidence for this exists in the famous Egyptian Amarna letters.

The Minoan Cretans had been part of the wider Bronze Age culture that existed in the Mediterranean and in the far west of Europe. We know from the work of J. Walter Graham that they used a measuring system that was clearly part of Megalithic 366° geometry, and that they had the ability and technology to track the Sun, Mercury and Venus with unerring accuracy.

On the other side of the coin we have a group of Enochian priests who are also likely to have been time-served astronomers, informed by the ancient knowledge of Enoch, which he himself had acquired at least partly in far-off Megalithic Ireland. Thus we have Megalithic influence coming into the region from two different directions at the very time the first Jerusalem Temple was planned and built.

There is a legend that the area that we now know as Jerusalem had been significant for many centuries before the Hebrews arrived and it is also suggested that treasures from the time of Enoch were discovered below the Mount when the foundations of the Temple were being dug. Included amongst these treasures was the 'golden chevron' about which I will have more to say presently.

The Old Testament would lead us to believe that, after the reign of Solomon, the Storm God of the Hebrews began to reign supreme and became the only deity of the Jewish people. But like other religious books, the Old Testament of the Bible was written or altered by a particular group of people at a specific period of history. Snippets of information through-out the Old Testament give us clues that Ashtoreth continued to be worshipped alongside Jehovah and there are instances when the pillars sacred to her had to be removed from shrines in the countryside, even from the Temple itself. I suggest that what happened subsequently, demonstrates that the importance of Ashtoreth was never lost to the Enochian priests, who had been influenced by the science and religion of the Megalithic peoples of the Mediterranean and Western Europe. They continued to use the zodiac that had originally been laid down in Crete, and to hold the planet Venus in great awe.

The expected Messiah, foretold by the appearance of such a significant Shekinah around AD 1, never materialized in the way people had hoped and expected. Instead, a flurry of new religious imperatives arose, suggesting that the nature of the expected Messiah was quite different to that so often prophesied. The Christians, for example, believed that, although Jesus had not taken up arms against the Romans, his rank as Messiah was relevant because he was God born in a human form.

It has to be remembered that the area of the Near East at this point in history was a melting pot of different beliefs and religious practices. The whole region was under the dominance of an occupying force. The Romans followed a wealth of different religions and this was reflected by a very cosmopolitan populace, especially in the area around Galilee. The worship of Isis was common in the area, as was that of Demeter, together with mystery cults such as that of Mithras and a sprinkling of offshoots of Messiah worship, such as Christianity and even a sect dedicated to Jesus' cousin, John the Baptist.

Political agitation was common and civil unrest was never far from the surface. It all finally exploded in AD 66, when a general uprising took place and hundreds of Roman soldiers were massacred across the region. At the time, the old Temple of Solomon in Jerusalem had just been rebuilt, at tremendous cost, by King Herod. But the splendid new building did not last long. Rome simply had to respond and the Emperor sent new legions to the area. In AD 70, Jewish Zealots took control of the Temple in Jerusalem, which was then besieged by Roman forces and eventually totally destroyed.

Thousands of people were killed in the Jewish uprisings and, until the creation of Israel in the 1940s, the Jews would never again have a homeland they could call their own. But many people did escape, amongst them some of the followers of the new cult of Christianity. Within this cult were the remnants of the Enochian priests, who ultimately found their way to the very frontiers of the Roman Empire, and especially to Gaul (now France). There they remained, but they did not forget their heritage, despite the passing centuries. They were biding their time, passing on their special knowledge from father to son and eventually becoming what we termed 'the Star Families'.

CHAPTER ELEVEN

HIDDEN IN PLAIN SIGHT

The Templar Treasures and their Journey

It is easy to see, with hindsight, what the Star Families wanted. It was their foremost desire once again to occupy and control Jerusalem, which they considered to be the holiest and most important city in the world. At first, as part of the Jewish uprising, many of the Enochian priests had been wanted men and, had their true background been discovered, they would quickly have been executed. Many probably were. The prospect of the developing Star Families ever reoccupying Jerusalem in the short term was unthinkable, and the Roman Empire still had several centuries to run.

What they could do was to travel far from the Near East and take refuge amongst the hotchpotch of faiths freely practised within the Roman world; and they were especially drawn to developing Christianity. It took quite a few centuries for Christianity to adopt its specifically *Catholic* flavour and any who think the path of modern Christianity was either logical or smooth knows little about the history of their religion.

What had originally been a purely local cult centred on Jerusalem soon took on a wider scope. Those who wished to prosper as Christian leaders had to offer their followers something that could compare with other cults and religions of the period. This is undoubtedly why aspects of Mithraism and especially the mystery religions of Demeter and Isis found their way into developing Christianity. The death and resurrection of Jesus can be seen as a replay of the dying and reborn Corn God, who was already familiar to the devotees of numerous faiths of the early Christian period. The story of Jesus offered a sound moral basis, becoming popular with people right across the social and economic spectrum and offering leaders a chance to secure and keep a degree of power over their followers.

Whether the Star Families pretended to follow the Christian faith prior to the adoption of Christianity by the Roman Empire is impossible to say, but there is no doubt that they did so after the event.

By the start of the 4th century AD, the Roman Empire was in a perilous state. It suffered from being too large and also from the constant infighting of those who wished to become its leaders. Client tribes within and on the edges of the Empire took the opportunity of a weakened infrastructure to rise up and attack the authorities, with the result that there were simply not enough legions available to deal with all the trouble simultaneously. Then one Roman emperor, or rather a would-be emperor, had an idea that turned out to be a stroke of genius. His name was Constantine and he decided that what the ailing Empire really needed was a common religious belief. This, he hoped, would become the cement that would hold the whole creaking edifice together.

Constantine committed the Roman world to Christianity in the 4th century AD, but he could easily have chosen some other religion. Mithraism was very strong and popular, but it tended to be restricted to soldiers and their families. Demeter was popular too but she was too Greek and Isis was too Egyptian. What Constantine required was a belief that anyone could embrace, but one that could be controlled by the state.

Christianity, which was already popular in many places throughout the

Empire, proved to be the best choice. After all, it already contained strong elements of the religions of Isis and Demeter, as well as aspects of Mithraism. It was itself a mystery religion, already developing a strong infrastructure that would be useful to the Empire. Christianity promised an afterlife and, what was more, an afterlife that depended on the behaviour of the individual while he or she was still living in this world. It would be relatively easy to hijack Christianity and to turn it to the needs of the state.

But before Constantine could really use Christianity, he first had to formalize it. There were too many contrasting sects within Christianity for it to be a useful and cohesive force for Roman rule. Some Christians believed that Jesus was the Son of God, while others held that he literally *was* God. Meanwhile, there were Christian sects that accepted the Virgin Mary as being as good as a goddess, whilst others suggested she was nothing more than a very blessed human being.

The differences went even further. There were Christian denominations that believed the whole world was inherently evil, or even suggested there were two gods, one who was manifested in the harsh, material world and another that existed only on a spiritual plane. Then there were the moderates, who accepted Jesus as a very special prophet but who rejected the mystery aspects of the religion as being built on superstition.

Constantine gathered all the Church leaders together and told them to sort things out. If they couldn't, he assured them, almost in as many words, he would do it himself. A power struggle followed and what emerged was something broadly akin to the Orthodox Christianity that is still practised in the east of Europe and the Middle East. True Catholicism would have to wait a few centuries before it emerged, but one thing was for sure; anyone who refused to toe the party line, once Constantine set his seal upon the Church, was likely to meet a sudden and nasty demise.

This seems to have suited the Star Families very well. We don't see them truly emerging again until around AD 1000 but, by the time they do

re-emerge, they are in positions of power and doing very well for themselves. They had ridden out the trials and tribulations associated with
the formalization of Christianity and coped with the gradual demise of the
Roman Empire. It seems obvious that these families had taken a conscious
decision to live both inside and outside the structures they were using to
gradually gain the power required to achieve their greatest objective, which
was to get back to Jerusalem.

It would not have been hard to pay lip service to Christianity – after
all, Christian iconography lends itself to a range of different beliefs. The
Virgin Mary gradually became so popular and important (probably with
the influence of the Star Families), that she took a central place in terms
of iconography and worship. In most churches her presence was far more
pronounced that that of God or Jesus. The saying goes that you can take a
horse to water but you can't make it drink. Similarly, you can see someone
who readily and regularly attends church but you can have no idea what
is going on in his or her mind or devotions. But as we will see, the Star
Families did not waver in their ultimate intentions and, generation by
generation, they secretly brought up their children to understand what
was required – though only when the time and circumstances were right.
Circumstances became right at the end of the first millennium AD.

Christianity at the end of the first millennium suffered from severe
competition. Islam, a religion that had sprung from similar Judaic roots,
was starting to spread, first through the Middle East, then out into the
Mediterranean.

Many of the Mediterranean islands fell to the Islamic invaders and
then, in 711, southern Spain was invaded and occupied, impinging on
mainland Europe. Meanwhile, other Islamic forces did their best to cut the
Christian world in half. They did not have to work too hard because the
Eastern and Western Churches had been divided for some time. By 1070
the situation became critical for Eastern Christianity, with its headquarters

in Constantinople coming under great pressure from Muslim invaders.

For most of the intervening centuries there was no love lost between the Eastern and Western branches of Christianity. The authorities in Rome showed no desire to heal the divisions of the past: to rush to the aid of the Eastern Church was unthinkable because, in the eyes of so many of the popes in Rome the Orthodox were not *real* Christians at all. But all this changed in 1071, and the alteration in events was down to one man. His name was Odo and he came from Lagery in Champagne, northern France.

We often tend to look at history in the light of specific events – the Norman Conquest of England, the storming of the Bastille in France or the attack by the Japanese on Pearl Harbour. Particular happenings can play a profound part in the way things turn out but, in the main, history is composed of *trends* rather than specific events. To take the last example, by the time the Pearl Harbour attack took place, the United States was well aware that war was imminent. Japan knew that the United States was mobilizing and dreamed up what turned out to be a rather unsuccessful pre-emptive strike to constrain America's ability to fight. War between the United States and Japan was already inevitable and the sequence of events that led to war went back decades. The attack on Pearl Harbour was one of a sequence of events, even though it is often viewed in stark isolation.

The same is true with regard to the series of Crusades that took place from the 11th century onwards. It was not simply the pleas of a beleaguered Eastern Church that led to thousands of men setting out to fight in foreign lands. Western Europe – in fact most of Europe at the time – was composed of feudal kingdoms where monarchs held ultimate power, bolstered by powerful families that owed fealty to the king. Below them were lesser aristocratic families that owed allegiance to the great lords, and so on, down the line to freemen, cottagers and peasants. The petty lords wanted to be more powerful and the great lords vied for ultimate supremacy and sometimes even for the throne.

Aristocrats had large families with many sons, all of whom wanted a slice of the feudal action. As a result, the amount of infighting and petty bickering was huge. It was nearly always those at the bottom of the social pyramid who suffered but, more significantly, the Church suffered too. Its property was damaged or destroyed and its priests were often caught up in civil unrest. In short, it disapproved of these mounted thugs charging about the countryside doing just what they wanted. Armed knights were the tanks of their day and they could do a tremendous amount of damage.

Successive prelates, especially throughout the 11th century, had despaired for their Church and the genuinely holy men within Christianity deplored the fact that so many innocent people were suffering. Popes longed for a way of getting rid of at least some of the aristocratic bullies, but there was little cohesion between the states of Europe, and the pope's influence was limited.

Genius sees a need and discovers a way to deal with it, while at the same time achieving one's own, personal objectives: this was demonstrated par excellence by the Star Families in 1071 and the decades that followed. For centuries the descendants of the Enochian priesthood had been living in various parts of the old Roman Empire. They had been extremely patient. There were not enough of them to launch an assault on Jerusalem and there never could be. Recognizing this, they strove instead for influence, both inside and outside the Church.

Though little-mentioned by historians, almost everything that inspired the First Crusade in the Near East came from a fairly tight area of northern France. In particular, the region of Champagne was pivotal in brokering the First Crusade, remaining significant throughout a crucial period of around three centuries. It was in this region, and specifically within the historic city of Troyes, that the Star Families had chosen to base most of their efforts. Generation by generation, members of the Star Families had intermarried into the aristocratic families of the region, and by the 11th century they had control of Champagne.

It would have been almost impossible for the Star Families to gain political control to achieve their primary objective of recapturing Jerusalem, but they might arrive at the same objective by the back door. What they required was to gain control of the one institution that was common to all of the Western states – the Church. In 1088 they achieved their objective when a man by the name of Odo of Lagery, one of their own, was elected as pope.

Odo came from Châtillon-sur-Marne, born of exactly the sort of aristocratic Champagne-based family that would nudge and manoeuvre events for decades. After a glittering career in the Church, Odo of Lagery was elected pope in March 1088, starting immediately to undertake the task he had been trained from childhood to work towards.

Pope Urban II, as Odo now was, made a passionate plea for a Crusade to be launched against Islam. In particular he called for an army to free Jerusalem of Islamic rule. His reason was that innocent Christian pilgrims were either being denied access to Jerusalem, or they were being harassed when they were there – though there is little evidence to show that this was the case.

But Pope Urban II was a passionate orator and he knew that there were thousands of armed knights available – mostly the younger sons of minor and middle-ranking nobility that were spoiling for a fight – any fight.

Help came from many different countries and eventually a great army was assembled, which fought its way to Jerusalem and ultimately besieged and captured the city in July 1099. First across the broken walls was a close kinsman of the Champagne families. His name was Godfrey de Bouillon and he came from Flanders. Godfrey became the first Christian ruler of Jerusalem and much of the Holy Land and, for a while at least, the Star Families had achieved their primary objective.

Shortly after, back in Champagne, the next stage of the plan was organized. Another member of the Star Families, a minor noble called Hugh de Payens, gathered together a group of eight knights, many of whom were also of aristocratic Champagne blood, and they arranged to set out to Jerusalem on a specific mission. He and his little band arrived there in 1119 and went straight to the then ruler of Jerusalem, a man blood-related to the Count of Champagne, and asked for his support. Hugh de Payens announced that he wanted to set up a military fighting force working exclusively for God. His aim, he claimed, was to protect pilgrims on the way to and from Jerusalem from the coastal ports.

Orthodox history, or at least folk tales from the time, tell us that the nine knights were impoverished, but nothing could be further from the truth. They were sponsored by the Count of Champagne, who later became one of their number, and they obviously had great influence with King Baldwin II of Jerusalem, who immediately granted them accommodation on the Temple Mount, right over the location of the Temple of Jerusalem.

As far as we can tell, not a single pilgrim was assisted by this little band of knights, who virtually disappeared from history for nine full years. So what were they doing during all this time, if not securing the safety of pilgrims? They were digging, gradually working their way down to the subterranean vaults below the Temple and into tunnels they knew existed there. How did they know? Their own ancestors were the priests who had safeguarded whatever lay beneath the Temple in the days before it was destroyed by the Roman legions.

After nine years the knights returned to Champagne to a hero's welcome. Their return was stage-managed by another of the Star Family representatives that had been placed in the Church and then allowed to develop great influence. His name was Bernard of Clairvaux, one of the most charismatic and ablest churchmen of his era and probably the most influential of all the 12th-century Star Family representatives.

Bernard had been born in the north of Burgundy, but his was an old Champagne family. As a young man he joined an infant monastic sect called the Cistercians. With him he took so many of his relatives and retainers that it was a foregone conclusion that they would swamp the new institution. This they did and Bernard rose like a rocket. In three short years he had his own monastery at Clairvaux, close to Troyes in the heart of Champagne. From here he continued to spread his influence throughout the Church and co-operated with other Star Family members who were running Champagne.

When the nine 'impoverished' knights returned from Jerusalem in 1129 they just happened to walk into the city at the time the pope, now Honorius II, convened a council there. It was no coincidence because Bernard of Clairvaux had arranged the whole thing. It was at the Council of Troyes that the little band of knights was made into an official monastic order, responsible to the pope alone. They would call themselves 'The Poor Knights of Christ and the Temple of Solomon', but history knows them as the Knights Templar.

Whatever those first dusty knights had found below the Temple Mount brought them instant power and great riches. Within a short time the Knights Templar became the most famous fighting force of the age. Quite soon it had a massive standing army and controlled property across the whole of Western Europe and beyond. People flocked to join the Templars or offer them land and money. Soon they had ships passing back and forth across the Mediterranean taking soldiers and supplies to the Holy Land.

Meanwhile, Bernard of Clairvaux built up the Cistercian Order, which became the most successful monastic order to grace the Catholic Church. Both organizations used new and revolutionary means to grow, while at home the region of Champagne became the most prosperous and successful location in Western Europe. Its international markets attracted merchants from across the known world and its economic power eclipsed that of France, of which it was nominally a part.

What really set apart these three components of the Star Family tripartite strategy was the way in which they used money and trade to further their objectives. The Templars were far from being just a bunch of holy soldiers. They became involved on a massive scale in international trade, virtually inventing banking, indulging in money lending and running the biggest fleet of merchant ships seen up to that time. The Templars owned and controlled entire towns and, even more importantly, because of their money-lending schemes, they also controlled the crowned heads of many states, who became deeply indebted to them.

The people behind the Templars and the Cistercians, who eventually controlled large parts of both Church and State, met in the shady recesses of the grand buildings in Troyes. They were clearly astute individuals, surely knowing that the hold the West had on the Holy Land was tenuous at best. Persuading the combined forces of Christendom to capture the Holy Land was one thing, but holding onto it was something completely different.

Large standing armies were expensive to maintain and, no matter how successful the Templars may have become, they could not hope to garrison the Holy Land on their own. Rulers across Europe eventually tired of the constant crusading, whilst the combined Islamic forces ranged against those trying to hold the Holy Land were growing stronger every year.

So it was that Jerusalem eventually fell back into Muslim hands in 1187 and the remainder of the mainland of the Levant was abandoned in 1191 with the fall of Acre. The Templars survived for over a century beyond the loss of the Holy Land and went from strength to strength, whilst the Cistercians continued to prosper and grow, creating their own economic power base within Western Christianity. During this period, Champagne continued to prosper and, through its powerful markets, it controlled much of the trade throughout Western Europe, beginning to evolve new financial strategies that would eventually change the feudal world forever.

It is particularly interesting to know that many of the systems of measure that eventually became the standard units in Britain, and eventually in the United States, owe their existence to the Champagne Fairs, as they were called. This is particularly true of measures of weight, such as the ounce and the pound. One such measure is still known as the 'Troy Ounce'. As we have seen, these were legacies of the ancient Megalithic system.

Even the mighty Knights Templar could not hold back time. Without a war to fight in the Near East, people began to ask why they continued to exist. They became hated as tax gatherers and the monarchs of Europe feared such a large standing army within their midst. It was rumoured that the Templars were planning to create a homeland of their own in Western Europe, and no king would have wanted the Templars for a neighbour.

When the region of Champagne came back into the hands of the French Crown at the end of the 13th century, the writing was on the wall for the Knights Templar. A particularly nasty and vindictive French king, Philip II, decided to deal with the Templars once and for all. He owed them a fortune, a debt that could be written off immediately if they ceased to exist.

The wily Philip hijacked the papacy, as the Star Families had themselves done three centuries earlier. With his own captive pope in place, in 1307 Philip moved against the Templars, accusing them of every sort of blasphemy, crime and impropriety. Nobody came to their aid and, officially at least, the Knights Templar were dissolved by the pope, ceasing to exist as a sanctioned religious order.

In reality this was not the case. As the Canadian writer Stephen Dafoe and I suggested in our book *The Warriors and the Bankers*, it is possible to cut off the head of a hydra but its writhing arms are not so easy to control. In all manner of guises, some virtually unchanged from their original form, the Templar organization lived on. Even if that had not been the case, as far as the feudal world was concerned the damage was already done. International trade on a huge scale, promoted by the Templars, the Cistercians and the powerful region of Champagne, had changed the world forever. The Star Families now had their hands on much of the wealth of Europe, which had been their primary objective from the start.

Whatever the first Templar knights had found below the Temple Mount never surfaced in public. It was probably kept at the Cathedral of Chartres in France, a wonderful cathedral masterminded and built with Templar influence and money. Alternatively, and in some ways even more likely, the Templar treasures were transhipped to Troyes. The cathedral of Troyes is magnificent, and it still holds some of the relics of Bernard of Clairvaux, now a saint.

But with Champagne losing its semi-autonomous status and France in the hands of an autocratic and ever more powerful dynasty of kings whose personal aims and objectives were much at odds with those of the Star Families, the treasure from the Temple Mount could not stay in France. It needed a new home and one that would be safe from the grasping and poor kings of France.

It is likely that the most important and significant items found by the Templars in Jerusalem left France in 1307 and were taken to the safety of the abbey of Kilwinning, in far-off Scotland, there to await the more permanent home that would be built specifically to house them.

The Star Families' desire to create their Heaven on Earth in Jerusalem had become a non-starter, but this did not cause them to abandon their overall intention. They had changed the world significantly and, through their efforts, the age of tyranny and feudalism had been dealt such a strong blow that it started to falter and would soon collapse. Patience was, and always had been, their middle name. If the capital of their new Heaven on Earth could not be Jerusalem, they would find somewhere else for it, somewhere not simply in a new country but in an entirely new continent.

CHAPTER TWELVE

THE TREASURE BOX
OF ROSSLYN

The Templars and the Birth of Freemasonry

On the morning of Friday 13 October 1307, the forces of King Philip II of France simultaneously entered every Templar property across France. These secret dawn raids had been calculated to avoid giving the Templars warning of what was to come. Philip wanted all the evidence he could find that the Templars were a heretical sect with strange practices, but more than this he wanted to lay his hands on as much Templar treasure as he could.

Philip must have been furious to discover that anything of value in the various Templar establishments, even the headquarters in Paris, had been removed. A good percentage of the personnel was also absent and, though the Grand Master, Jacques de Molay, was captured, together with some of his high-ranking officers, a great many of the Templars in France had simply disappeared.

The Templar fleet of ships, moored at La Rochelle, had quietly slipped anchor on the night of 12 October and simply sailed out of history. The Templars were not taken by surprise and King Philip II was something of a fool for expecting that they could be. Philip had telegraphed every one of his moves and he could not possibly have acted against the Templars all over France without giving them warning because they almost certainly had spies everywhere.

Stephen Dafoe and I showed in *The Warriors and the Bankers* and *The Templar Continuum* that most of the Templar money that wasn't tied up in transactions all over Europe was almost certainly moved east, into the Alps. There the Templars helped to create the very peculiar state of Switzerland, which freed itself of any form of domination by other powers. Whatever the Templars took to Switzerland in the way of assets was quite safe there, but the most important artefacts they had recovered from beneath the Temple Mound were not transhipped to Switzerland, but rather in the opposite direction.

There is, and always has been, a persistent rumour that the Templar fleet, escaping on the night of 12 October 1307, headed for Scotland. This is understandable. Robert the Bruce, the Scottish king, had no love for the papacy and was on good terms with the Templars. But the thought of the entire Templar fleet going t ⟩ Scotland is absurd. Many of the ships at La Rochelle were of a type completely unsuited to the weather conditions in the North Sea, created specifically for the Mediterranean. Any large fleet setting sail to Scotland from La Rochelle could not have escaped the attention of English ships that patrolled the coast of Britain.

The origins of the myth that the Templars escaped to Scotland most likely originates from one or two Templar ships making this journey in October 1307 or maybe somewhat earlier. Piecing together all available information, and working on Freemasonic stories, it seems that the ultimate destination of these ships was the west coast of Scotland and the port of Irvine, close to which was the town of Kilwinning.

During my investigations into the story of the Templars, both with Stephen Dafoe and Chris Knight, no monastic order from the period has intrigued me more than the Tironensians. This little-remembered monastic order was a near contemporary of the Cistercians, originating in more or less the same part of France. Its leader was another Bernard, this time Bernard of Ponthieu. Ponthieu is a village near Abbeville in Normandy. This Bernard, also known as Bernard of Thiron, like his namesake Bernard of Clairvaux, sought a form of monasticism freed from the pomp and riches of the Benedictine order and so, after quite a few adventures, he formed a new order in Thiron, near Chartres.

From the very start the Tironensian monks became manual labourers specializing in building. The spectacular growth of the Cistercian order was amazing enough but that of the Tironensians, at least at first, was even more startling. Within five years of its creation the order had 117 priories and abbeys in France, England, Wales, Scotland and Ireland.

The order was tremendously influential in its time and may have been primarily responsible for the introduction of the famous Gothic style of architecture. It taught stonemasonry to its novices but also had schools of architecture for those who were not monks, most notably in Chartres. The Tironensians were undoubtedly the genius behind the building of remarkable Chartres Cathedral.

Discovering much regarding the Tironensians is extremely difficult because their existence seems to have been all but expunged from history. But we do know that in Scotland they first built Selkirk Abbey in 1113, Kelso Abbey in 1128 and Kilwinning Abbey in 1140. It is at Kilwinning that many Scottish Freemasons claim their Craft originated. The Freemasonic lodge in Kilwinning has a unique distinction. Because of its great age and its claims to being the very first Masonic lodge, it is known as 'Lodge 0' to distinguish it from 'Lodge 1' in Edinburgh, Scotland's capital.

As far as the Kilwinning Freemasons are concerned, there is no doubt about their own story. Kilwinning Abbey was founded by the Tironensians in 1140 and a Masonic lodge was present there in the Chapter House from the very start. It continued to meet in the Chapter House until 1540 when, with the Reformation, the abbey was sacked.

But how could this be the case? It is known that the Tironensians were involved in training people outside the order in the art of architecture and building, and the order would have needed more stonemasons than could be supplied from within its own ranks. As a result, it is entirely possible that stonemasons did meet regularly in the abbey to receive instruction and to become part of the 'Lodge' or guild set up by the monks. The Tironensians supervised the building of many parish churches across Scotland, and this too may well have been organized at Kilwinning.

Chris Knight and I came to the conclusion that items from below the Temple Mount in Jerusalem did find their way to the Abbey of Kilwinning. It is not out of the question that these items were brought to Scotland almost as soon as they were brought back to Western Europe. After the Council of Troyes in 1128 the leaders of the newly sanctioned Templars went straight to Scotland, where it is said Hugh de Payens already owned land. It may be a coincidence that Kelso Abbey was constructed in the same year the Council of Troyes took place, but it is equally possible that it was constructed specifically to hold whatever the Templars had brought back with them from Jerusalem.

Kelso is close to the English border and the Scots, as was often the case, were not on good terms with the English, so it was probably considered prudent to move the treasures to a less accessible place, once Kilwinning Abbey was built in 1140.

On the other hand, the Templar treasures may not have arrived in Kilwinning until Champagne came under threat. Either way, it seems to be the case that they did end up at Kilwinning, before being transhipped again to a new home created for them in Scotland.

This brings us to Rosslyn Chapel, one of the strangest and most enigmatic structures ever to be created in the British Isles. Rosslyn Chapel is supposed to be a church but, if so, it is a most unusual one.

It was commenced around 1446 and it took a reported 40 years to complete, which might lead one to believe that this is a significantly large structure, but Rosslyn Chapel is actually quite small. It is located not far from Edinburgh and was built by William St Clair, third Earl of Orkney and was, at least supposedly, the first part of a much larger project to build an entire collegiate church. It has been suggested that what we see at the site today is merely the Lady Chapel and that the rest of the church was never completed.

The St Clairs were a formidable family in Scotland. They had been in the country for centuries before Rosslyn Chapel was created. Thanks to shrewd actions and judicious marriages they had become one of the wealthiest and most powerful dynasties. Unlike other baronial Scottish families the St Clair clan was always unswervingly loyal to the Scottish kings and gained great favour as a result.

Legend asserts that William St Clair's grandfather, Henry St Clair, had organized a transatlantic voyage, or maybe more than one, long before Christopher Columbus made his way across the Atlantic. This would not be out of the question. Henry St Clair had Norse blood in his veins and it is generally accepted that the Vikings visited North America on a number of occasions.

It is also suggested that the St Clair family had close ties to the Knights Templar. This is difficult to prove, but it would be strange if they did not. Practically all the major families across Europe contributed sons to the Templar order and the Templars certainly did have establishments on St Clair land in Scotland. What is more significant is that the St Clairs had Star Family credentials. They came originally from northern France, retaining good connections with exactly the sort of individuals who stand out as being our chief suspects for carrying Star Family objectives forward across many centuries.

Rosslyn Chapel is a veritable 'confection in stone'. If there are churches of the period that carry more carvings per square yard, I have not seen them. This small, squat and somewhat dark little building is not actually like a church at all. Upon entering, one immediately gets the impression it is a temple. The building has a barrel-vaulted roof, replete with dozens of gold stars, suns and moons, and its stonework in every nook and cranny, inside and out, is alive with carvings of every conceivable sort. To understand what the stonemasons were trying to impart with all these creations is almost impossible and it is really a case of isolating small parts of the chapel rather than trying to make sense of everything at once.

I had been friends for 12 years with a man born and raised in the village just outside the chapel, who has made a lifetime study of the site. In 2005 we decided to pool our resources and to take an in-depth look at Rosslyn Chapel with a view to finally unlocking some of its secrets. John Ritchie knows more about Rosslyn Chapel, its legends, its timeline and its significance than any other living individual and our co-operation resulted in the 2006 book *Rosslyn Revealed*.

Previous to our investigations, Chris Knight and Robert Lomas had come to their own conclusions regarding the chapel. In their book *The Hiram Key* they suggested that Rosslyn Chapel was deliberately built as a copy of part of King Solomon's Temple in Jerusalem. They made a convincing case, and there are carvings within the chapel itself that bear out their assertion. They went on to suggest that Rosslyn Chapel was the repository of Templar artefacts recovered from Jerusalem. They also showed how strong the connections were between Rosslyn Chapel and the origination of Freemasonry.

Their ultimate conclusion was that William St Clair, who built the chapel, created Freemasonry as a way of keeping his masons quiet about aspects of the chapel that were clearly not Christian in origin and also regarding what had been buried in chambers or tunnels under the fabric of the building.

John Ritchie and I tried to avoid any preconceptions as we embarked on our own investigation of the building and, as a result, we immediately began to see things that other researchers had not. With my experience in ancient astronomy I recognize an observatory when I see one, and it wasn't long before I realized that, in part at least, this is what the chapel represents.

The building is situated close to the edge of a deep ravine, with its eastern end looking out across the valley to a distant horizon. At the eastern end of the chapel is the part of the building that is used as its altar. Above this is an almost flat roof, much lower than the roof of the chapel itself. I have stood on this platform, which is surrounded on the north, east and west by pinnacled crenulations. The view from this platform to the east is uninterrupted and it seemed to me that the spacing of the pinnacled crenulations was such that they had been created for the purpose of tracking a large proportion of the eastern sky.

Rosslyn Chapel is dedicated to St Matthew, which is not odd in itself until one realizes that the feast of St Matthew is celebrated in the West on 21 September. Anyone who has studied medieval churches soon becomes aware that, although the altar end of most churches faces east, roughly towards Jerusalem, there are many different versions of east represented. This is because many, if not most, of these churches were commenced on the feast day of the saint to which they were to be dedicated. As we have seen, the Sun changes its position at dawn on the eastern horizon throughout the year. So sunrise in high summer will be well north of east, whereas in midwinter it will be significantly south of east. Churches were invariably orientated towards sunrise on the feast day of their particular saint and not to true east.

Since Rosslyn Chapel was dedicated to St Matthew, whose feast day is also the autumn equinox, it is orientated due east, as was the viewing platform of Solomon's Temple in Jerusalem. Like Solomon's Temple, Rosslyn Chapel enjoys a particular place on the Earth in terms of the yearly sunrise pattern. In Jerusalem the Sun, at its extremes, rises at exactly 30° north or south of east, whereas in Rosslyn, significantly further north, the Sun's extremes stand at exactly 45° north or south of east. Both occurrences are significant in terms of geometry and create specific shadow patterns.

John and I discovered that, above the great east window of Rosslyn Chapel, its builders incorporated a glass box that passes through the fabric of the building and emerges above the window, high in the chapel at the east end. This produces a particular effect inside the building, which had been spoken about as a legend but never seen in living memory because it only takes place at dawn on two days of the year.

On the mornings of the spring and autumn equinoxes the Sun, having appeared on the eastern horizon, casts its light down this glass tube, coloured red, then emerging into the chapel. As a result, if there is a clear sky, a blood-red light shines into the body of the chapel at dawn on both these days. This is impressive and somehow quite unnerving. It is an artificially created version of the Shekinah that was so important to those who created the Temple in Jerusalem.

The reader will also recall that, in Washington DC, the Capitol was created on a north–south axis, so that its main entrance faces due east. As in Washington, when the Sun rises at Rosslyn on St Matthew's Day, 21 September, it is at the end of the zodiac sign of Virgo. There are therefore striking similarities between Solomon's Temple in Jerusalem, Rosslyn Chapel and Washington DC's Capitol.

In short, no structure I have ever seen better exemplifies the beliefs of the Star Families than this strange little building in Scotland. From the platform above the eastern end it would have been, and still is, possible to accurately track the patterns of sunrise and moonrise, as well as to monitor the behaviour of Venus and Mercury in a way that had been going on in Britain since the super-henges were created as far back as 3500 BC.

With regard to the assertion that Freemasonry began at Rosslyn, I don't doubt it for a minute. The abbey at Kilwinning, where the Templar treasures were stored when first brought to Scotland, lay on land owned by William St Clair. He would have been on good terms with the Tironensian monks and it seems to me that it was their knowledge, dedication and skill that went into the creation of Rosslyn Chapel. Clearly, whatever had been kept safe at Kilwinning Abbey could not have been brought to Rosslyn Chapel without the knowledge and co-operation of the monks.

Rosslyn Chapel is like a compendium of Gothic architecture. Small as it is, it contains almost every type of Gothic arch imaginable and it was clearly created by people at the very top of their game.

William St Clair had a vested interest in keeping his workers quiet about the real motivation behind the building of Rosslyn Chapel. All sorts of peculiarities must have been self-evident to them. For example, at the western end of the building the stonework has the look of a set of broken teeth, apparently because this ragged stonework was meant to key into the rest of the building when it was eventually created.

But experts called in by Chris Knight and Robert Lomas were absolutely certain that nothing else ever had been *seriously* intended. They declared Rosslyn Chapel to be a folly, a structure meant to stand alone, never intended to be any bigger than it is. The stonemasons who created the chapel cannot have been ignorant of this.

In addition, our investigations indicated that, although the site of the chapel was active from 1446, the cornerstone of the building was not actually laid until 21 September 1456. Clearly the foundations did not take 10 years to complete and there may be almost as much to Rosslyn Chapel below the ground as there is above it. It is most likely that, during the missing 10 years when the tunnels and passages were created, the stonemasons must have known of their existence.

William St Clair built an entire village for his workers, now known by the more modern spelling of Roslin. It wasn't simply a temporary hamlet because William had petitioned the King of Scotland to give the place a charter and a market. William undertook to look after his workers and he even arranged other contracts for them once the chapel was finished. In return he asked of them complete secrecy regarding the project. If the Vatican had really known what was going on at Rosslyn the St Clair family might have been in serious trouble. In order to secure the necessary silence from his workers William St Clair borrowed the ceremonies from the Tironensians that had evolved at Kilwinning and elsewhere.

Added to the existing rituals of what was essentially a guild, William St Clair brought aspects of the mysteries to bear on his new 'association'. He devised degrees of initiation, according to experience and trustworthiness, introducing threats of physical retribution for anyone who betrayed the chapel's secrets. Nobody ever did and, in all probability, none but the most experienced and intelligent of the masons could have done so.

With the passing of time the institution created by William St Clair continued to fascinate people. It was so popular that eventually it began to allow membership to people who were not stonemasons at all. Such was its popularity that it eventually spread to the nearby capital of Edinburgh, and the rest is history. Freemasonry was born.

For some years now the whole Chapel has been covered by a giant steel canopy, so that the stonework could be dried out and treated with chemicals to keep it sound for centuries to come. At the time of writing, the canopy is at last being removed. It means that visitors can see the chapel as it is meant to be seen, but it is also a little sad. Whilst the canopy was in place the owners of the chapel thoughtfully incorporated a walkway that took visitors above the ground so that they could see the chapel at waist height. Had it not been for this, it is unlikely that John Ritchie and I would have discovered the fantastic light box above the east window or recognized the observation platform for what it truly is. The removal of the walkway also means that visitors will not be able to appreciate the intricacy of Rosslyn Chapel's carvings high up on its exterior. It is a mark of respect to those who created the structure that these carvings, almost impossible to see from the ground, are as finely detailed and as excellent as anything inside the building.

As a safe and secure refuge for the Templar treasures, Rosslyn Chapel only lasted three or four centuries. By the time it was built, the writing was already on the wall for Catholicism as a major force in Britain, and it was within Catholicism that the Star Families had taken refuge, moulding it to their own purposes.

With the 16th century came the Reformation across Western Europe. In England it was inspired by the actions of King Henry VIII, but it took place in Scotland too and the forces of Protestantism soon made places such as Rosslyn into something of an anachronism. The sumptuous carvings and iconography of the chapel may never have been intended to represent traditional Catholic Christianity, but they could certainly be seen as such, and yet there is no indication that the St Clair family fell under the gaze of the Inquisition.

Protestantism, and especially Scottish Protestantism, was a different matter altogether. The puritanical Protestants disliked any sort of ornamentation and, in the time of Henry VIII, much of it was destroyed. Some fine churches did survive intact and Rosslyn Chapel was an example.

Ultimately the chapel fell into a state of disrepair, though it was undoubtedly safer that way. It lost part of its roof and most of its glass. It may have crumbled away altogether had it not been for Queen Victoria, who visited the place not long into her reign. She was enchanted by the building and suggested that it should be restored and re-opened as a place of worship. How opportune this must have seemed to the Star Families, who already had very different ideas regarding their 'New Jerusalem' and who had been working feverishly to create it anew in a very different environment, far away across the ocean.

CHAPTER THIRTEEN

THE NEW JERUSALEM

The Initiation of a Nation

Just across the Potomac from the Lincoln Monument is a district of Washington DC that is, to this day, called Rosslyn. It seems impossible to ascertain how it came to be so called but it isn't out of the question that when the artefacts from beneath the Temple Mount were first brought to the site they were kept, for a while at least, in the district that carries the same name as the chapel.

The most likely date for the transfer of the items is between1860 and 1862. At this time James Alexander St Clair-Erskine, then owner of Rosslyn Chapel, employed Freemasonic architect, David Bryce, to carry out restoration work on the chapel. The work was completed and the chapel rededicated in April 1862. This date marks a watershed in the life of Rosslyn Chapel, which was almost certainly never intended to be a *real* chapel, even if previously used as one.

When Bryce arrived at Rosslyn the chapel was in a sorry state. Much of the roof was missing, virtually all the windows had gone and the interior of the chapel was open to the elements. It is suggested that the floor was lifted and re-laid during the alterations, and the presence of a Freemasonic architect supervising whatever took place would ensure that absolute secrecy was maintained regarding whatever was removed from the site.

The placing of the recovered items in a vault planned for them in Washington DC could not take place in 1862 because the United States was at the time spiralling down into civil war. The creation of the Ellipse and probably the chamber dug below it had to wait for almost another decade, which is why it is most likely that the items brought from Scotland were kept in a temporary resting place, across the Potomac in Rosslyn.

With the war over, and plenty of soldier-engineers to do the work, the Ellipse was planned and created, along with other remedial work necessary to put Washington DC back in order after the disruptions. Lieutenant Colonel Thomas Lincoln Casey reported in 1878 that he could not access the centre of the Ellipse because work was being carried out there under the supervision of the District Commissioners, so this is the most likely time that the chamber was being prepared, under the guise of creating new sewers.

Eventually the work was finished and the Ellipse was set apart as part of President's Park, with a view to allowing public access for specific functions, for baseball and other games, so that locals could take some healthy exercise. Immediately to the north of the Ellipse a stone was placed representing the spot from which all subsequent mileages in the United States were to be taken. This same stone also marks the original north–south line intended to be the United States prime meridian.

Putting the Temple artefacts in this particular location was typical of Star Family actions. It simply could not be more public but, at the same time, it is well hidden and the land into which the chamber was dug will never be developed in any way. If even suggested that real estate could be built on part of, or the entire, Ellipse there would be a huge public outcry. The park is considered to be one of Washington DC's treasures and any buildings placed there would overlook the White House and spoil the view from the rear of the White House, down towards the Potomac and the Jefferson Monument.

Only a small handful of people would have known what was happening at the centre of the Ellipse in the 1870s. The two presidents in power during the decade were Ulysses S. Grant and Rutherford B. Hayes. It is not known whether either of them were Freemasons but there were plenty of high-ranking Freemasons in both administrations.

Allowing for the placement of the Capitol on its hill and the necessary measurements around the original right-angled triangle upon which the city was built, the centre of the Ellipse was considered to be the very centre of the District of Columbia, and as such could also be considered to be the spiritual centre of the United States. Only something of inestimable value would have been vouchsafed to this location.

The consignment must have been expected from the very foundation of Washington DC because the whole city was planned with this particular location in mind. The fact that the Ellipse makes Megalithic-style connections with so many circles and intersections, as well as with the Capitol and other structures I will mention presently, demonstrates that this is no *arbitrary* piece of ground that simply happened to be available. The great and complex arrow, described in Chapter 8, was also a legacy of the original planning of Washington DC and had been pointing to this particular spot long before the Ellipse was even laid out.

What went on behind the high, whitewashed fence on the White Lot before the Ellipse was created we have no way of knowing. It isn't out of the question that the necessary chamber had already been dug and prepared before the Civil War and that all that was necessary when the Ellipse was created was to place the artefacts in the chamber and seal it up again.

What might actually lie below the Ellipse I will deal with in the last chapter of this book, but it is interesting to note that the same careful Megalithic planning that went into Washington DC, both in terms of the diamond of Columbia and the layout of the city, was not forgotten in the intervening years. This realization was a shock to Chris Knight and myself when we were researching *Before the Pyramids*.

There is one building within the old boundaries of Washington DC that is so large and so iconic that we simply could not ignore it, though as we carefully measured its dimensions and the relative distances between it and other structures in the city we could hardly have expected to find anything of note. But in the end a close look at the Pentagon not only confirmed everything we had discovered but made it obvious that the Megalithic influences present when Washington DC was born were still in place as recently as 1940.

The Pentagon is the result of a very real need on the part of the United States to create a headquarters for its defence forces with almost no notice and in a very short space of time. As 1940 approached, the United States was recovering from one of the worst recessions ever to hit the West. With the help of the President, Franklin D. Roosevelt, the United States was on the way back to full employment and on the verge of becoming one of the most important and largest economies in the world.

America had adopted a generally isolationist policy after the First World War, which had seen many of her young men travel far across the ocean to die on a foreign shore with little or nothing to do with the United States itself. US involvement in the First World War may or may not have been a necessity, but many people told themselves that, whether or not it was a *cause célèbre*, the United States should now avoid getting itself involved in Europe's wars.

Franklin D. Roosevelt had ridden this isolationist policy and announced publically on more than one occasion that the sons of the United States would not be called upon to fight someone else's war again. Even when America's parent country, Britain, was brought to war with Germany in 1939, America refused to become involved – at least at first.

But the writing was on the wall. Japan was expanding at the far side of the Pacific, threatening to tread on the toes of US Pacific interests.

Roosevelt had not stood idly by whilst Japan sought to increase its influence by force, and to increase its abilities to gain the absolutely necessary raw materials it did not possess within the home islands. Embargos were put on Japan by the US. Anyone in the know gradually came to the conclusion that, with Europe in flames and Japan flexing its muscles, it was only a matter of time before the United States was drawn into another bloody war.

As the 1940s approached, the United States began to re-arm and to supply Britain with the materials it needed to prosecute its war against Germany. The draft was reintroduced and, to cope with the number of soldiers who would be gradually arriving for training, new forts and military installations sprang up all over the United States.

This took coordination, which was difficult when so many of the military headquarters were spread around in buildings all over Washington DC. The United States needed one cohesive headquarters, where all of its armed capabilities could be planned. So it was that a site was chosen at Arlington Farms and a suitable building was designed. But at the very last minute, in fact, only one day before the first turf was to be lifted on the site, President Roosevelt threw a spanner in the works by saying that the new military headquarters would have to be built somewhere else, specifically in Foggy Bottom, further south and by the side of the Potomac, though still on the far shore of the river.

The decision was not taken lying down. Brigadier General Brehon Sommervell, who was in charge of the project, did not relish interference from the White House and argued long and hard with Franklin Roosevelt that the original site was better and that it was too late to make such huge changes. The President would brook no interference and pulled rank by asking: 'Who is Commander in Chief of the United States Armed Forces?' Roosevelt got his way.

It was suggested at the time, and since, that President Roosevelt was responding to the worries of his uncle, Frederick A. Delano, an influential member of the National Capital Park and Planning Commission, that the new military headquarters, if placed at Arlington Farms, would obscure the view of Washington DC from Arlington National Cemetery.

It was on these grounds that the President chose to relocate the structure at the last minute, though it is very unlikely to have been the real reason. The original building had been proposed to have five sides, to accommodate road junctions at Arlington Farms, but although it remained five-sided in the change of plan, it became much more regular in shape and owed much of its ultimate design to the ideas of President Roosevelt, who was a keen amateur architect.

As it turned out the ultimate dimensions of the Pentagon, together with its overall shape and positioning, represent one of the greatest coups of the Star Families in modern times. Everything about it proves that the Megalithic knowledge that had gone into planning Washington DC had not been forgotten at all in the nearly two centuries that had elapsed since Pierre Charles L'Enfant had unrolled his first sheet of paper in the 18th century.

We looked at the Pentagon with little expectation but, in a few hours, we both stared in utter disbelief at what met our gaze. First of all we measured the distances between the centre of the Pentagon and the centre of the Ellipse Park. There was no doubt we were looking at another instance of a distance that could be resolved to units of 366MY. The distance from the Pentagon centre to the Ellipse centre is 3,036 metres (9,960ft). This is 10×366MY, to an incredible degree of accuracy. Meanwhile the distance from the centre of the Pentagon to the Capitol is 4,554 metres (1,491ft), which is 15×366MY.

Since there is a Megalithic connection between the centre of the Ellipse and the Capitol, which are 2,429 metres (7,969ft) apart, leading to a measurement of 8×366MY, the three sites taken together form a large Megalithic triangle with an overall distance around its three sides of 33×366MY. The significance of this will become obvious presently.

As if this wasn't enough, the actual size of the Pentagon was even more informative and surprising. All regular pentagons, such as this one, are created within a circle. The circle around the Pentagon measures 1,830MY in circumference, which means that the gap between each corner of the building and its neighbour, around this circle, is exactly 366MY. Could this possibly be true? We measured the building time and again, on Google Earth and on large-scale maps. There was no doubt about it. The Pentagon is a totally Megalithic building.

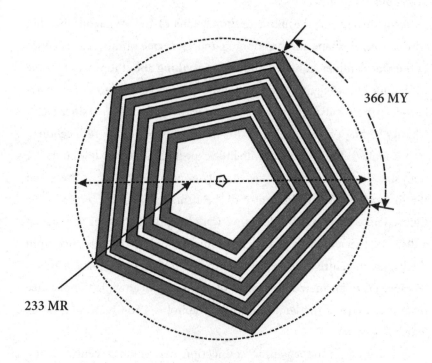

circle diameter = 233MR, circle circumference = 732MR
or 5×366MY (MY=82.966cm, MR=207.415cm)

Figure 30. The Dimensions of the Pentagon, Washington DC

Just as important, if not more so, is the fact that the diameter of the circle into which the Pentagon was built is 233 Megalithic Rods. (A Megalithic Rod is another measurement rediscovered by Professor Alexander Thom. The Megalithic Rod is 2.5 times the length of the Megalithic Yard.)

We were absolutely blown away by this measurement because it conforms to something we observed way back when we wrote *Before the Pyramids*. We had expected the Megalithic builders to be fascinated by any circle with a diameter of 233 units because such a circle must have a circumference of 732 of the same units, and 732 is twice 366. We called this circle a 'pi survivor' because it is one of very few circles in which both the diameter and the circumference can be expressed in whole numbers of the same units, to an accuracy of 99.999 per cent.

There can be no doubt that whoever decided on the final dimensions of the Pentagon in Washington DC had a very good understanding of the basic linear measurements of the Megalithic system. Such absolutely accurate measurements as these simply could not have come about by chance.

The reason the designers could get away with these Megalithic measurements without anyone thinking there was something odd taking place was that all the Megalithic figures relate to a circle that is theoretical, rather than actual. In other words, the circle does not exist on the ground but is merely the starting point for creating the Pentagon itself.

So, like the Megalithic Yard inside Thomas Jefferson's intended system of measurements, the Megalithic Yard and the Megalithic Rod are present, but hidden in plain sight. However, of the relationship between the Pentagon, the centre of the Ellipse and the Capitol there is no doubt. It definitely comes out at 33×366MY.

So, how is this number significant and what does it mean to Washington DC and the United States as a whole? Actually, it is very telling and relates specifically to Freemasonry. This is perhaps not too surprising because

Franklin D. Roosevelt was a keen Freemason and had been so for most of his adult life. In the United States the most popular form of Freemasonry is known as 'Scottish Rite' Freemasonry. In addition to the three usual degrees – Entered Apprentice, Fellowcraft and Master Mason – it has additional degrees, each with its own distinctive name, ceremonies and symbols. In all, there are 33 degrees in Scottish Rite Freemasonry and President Roosevelt held them all.

It just so happens that the symbol for the 32nd degree of Scottish Rite Freemasonry is a pentagon, whilst the symbol for the 33rd degree is a triangle. It doesn't take much imagination to see what is going on here. The construction of the Pentagon completed the 32nd degree as far as Washington DC is concerned – and in fact, by implication, as far as the United States is concerned too.

At the same time its connections with the Ellipse centre and the Capitol created a triangle that symbolized the highest 33rd degree of the Scottish Rite. To drive the point home, the distance around this triangle equals 33×366MY. This is not 33 Megalithic degrees of the Earth's circumference, which would be absolutely massive, but is a symbolic 1×360th of 33 actual Megalithic degrees of the Earth's circumference. These numbers are all highly symbolic in the Megalithic system.

If all of this isn't enough, we only have to look at the ceremony associated with the 32nd degree of Scottish Rite Freemasonry, known as 'The Master of the Royal Secret'. All the Scottish Rite degrees have an allegory attached to them – a story or a short play that encompasses the true importance of the particular degree in question. We explained the 32nd degree allegory in detail in *Before the Pyramids*.

Briefly, the person wishing to be a 32nd degree Mason takes on the persona of a knight by the name of Constans. In the allegory Constans is left alone at the altar of a cathedral, in lonely vigil in the night before his raising to the rank of 'Master of the Royal Secret'. He has been told that he must keep the vigil no matter what, and that if he falters or leaves his place at the altar he can never be considered a true Master of the Royal Secret.

On several occasions Constans is tempted to leave the cathedral, either on the pretext of enjoying himself or because he needs to attend to worldly duties, but on each occasion he stands fast. Eventually he hears the noise of fighting beyond the doors of the cathedral and hears shouts that indicate the pentagon-shaped camp has been attacked and his leader is slain. It is at this point that Constans realizes that he cannot keep his vigil any longer. This is what he says:

> What is that? An alarm? Can it be a treacherous assault?
> Or is it only another trial of my fidelity? What shall I do?
> I was admonished to keep my vigil, but the city is in peril.
> They told me I must stay here. All my future depends on
> my obedience. But how can I stay while children may be
> murdered and women ravished? No, I cannot stay! I must go.

He goes on to say:

> Our leader is slain! And I am here in cowardly safety. My
> people are in peril; I must go. My hope is in God.

Grasping his sword he rushes out into the battle. After a few moments the assembly of characters who were present at the start of the scene return. The battle is apparently won, thanks to the intervention of one particularly powerful and brave knight. All present are astonished to see that Constans is missing from his vigil and make the assumption that he had fled in fright.

It is at this point that four men enter, carrying a bier upon which is laid the body of Constans. All present now realize that Constans was the brave knight who saved the city and they show their remorse at having considered him a coward. They declare that Constans does not need to be told the Royal Secret, because he surely knows it already. It is at this point that the allegory ends.

Now let us look again at what was taking place in America when the Pentagon was built. After a protracted period during which the United States had looked in upon itself, and when it had steadfastly refused to become involved in conflicts outside its own shores, the country was now beginning to realize that this course of action would be difficult to maintain and probably morally impossible to justify. Constans rushed out to defend his mother, his sister, his brothers and, just as importantly, people he did not personally know, because according to the rules and observances of Freemasonry, these people too were his kin. Now the United States was readying itself to embark upon another ghastly war, but one that was being waged to defend the cause of freedom. The parallel is not difficult to draw.

Those in authority in the United States, amongst whom President Roosevelt was clearly a leading player, created the Pentagon and decided where and what it was to be in order to complete both the 32nd degree and the 33rd degree of Scottish Rite Freemasonry on behalf of every citizen of the United States of America.

This carries some important implications. The allegory being played out was 100 per cent Freemasonic, but it was employed in full knowledge of the ancient Megalithic system of measurements. We cannot therefore doubt a direct connection between the Star Families and American Freemasonry. They may not be exactly the same thing, but there is clearly a connection, both in terms of intention and belief.

Nor did these two groups forget the sacrifice that was made by Americans all over the world during the Second World War. The newest structure to take its place on the Mall in Washington DC is the National World War II Memorial. It is located between the Washington Monument and the

Lincoln Memorial, on the site of the older Rainbow Pool. Several sites were proposed when it was first discussed at committee in 1995, but the site of the Rainbow Pool was soon selected. Work on the memorial began in September 2001 and the monument was dedicated on April 2004.

The site chosen for the World War II Memorial is not arbitrary. The centre of the oval structure is 607 metres (1,992ft) from the centre of the Ellipse, which is 2×366MY. But the memorial also forms a triangle of its own, similar to the triangle formed by the Ellipse, the Capitol and the Pentagon. In the case of the World War II Memorial triangle, the total distance around its three sides is 9,716 metres. That means it is equal to 32×366MY, which brings us again to the 32nd degree allegory concerning Constans and his selfless sacrifice. How absolutely appropriate this is.

This monument is the monument for Constans of the 32nd degree – and in reality all the embodiments of Constans who gave their lives to help their brothers and sisters, in the United States and across the world. Step back and think about this for a moment. Is there even the remotest chance that any of this could be a haphazard coincidence?

In the meantime the 33rd degree was also conferred upon the United States once the Pentagon was in place and the final symbol of Freemasonry was established. This is the triangle, which in this case runs from the Capitol to the Ellipse centre, then on to the Pentagon centre and back to the Capitol – a true 33 Megalithic Second of arc triangle for a 33rd-degree honour. In truth there are many 33rd-degree Freemasons, but to most the degree is offered as an honorary statement of deeds done, either for Freemasonry or for society.

But beyond the ex-presidents, civil servants, bankers and bus drivers who might have had this honour bestowed upon them, there are 33 other men who hold the 33rd-degree title, and to whom it really does mean something. These are the 33 men that make up the Supreme Council of American Scottish Rite Freemasonry. Each is specifically chosen, though nobody knows how or why, and at their head is one, super-elevated Freemason who runs the entire show. Chris and I were told by a friend of his, who has the 33rd-degree honorary status, that the Scottish Rite is by no means a democracy. Everything is decided by a Supreme Council, without recourse to the brothers lower down the tree, and the Supreme Council itself is generally responsive to the wishes of its most elevated member.

What we should not forget is that when the Pentagon opened for business on 15 January 1943, the whole of Washington DC, and therefore the United States, took on the mantle of the 33rd degree, the title of which is Inspector General. It seems to me to be self-evident that, when this took place, those ruling the United States, and especially the high-ranking Scottish Rite Freemasons amongst them, took this as a signal that the United States henceforth became 'Inspector General' of the world. The days of isolation were gone and the world's foremost superpower came into existence. History has since proved conclusively that the United States takes its role as Inspector General of the world very seriously indeed.

As I mentioned earlier, anyone who doubts the idea that the United States is fully behind the creation of a new world order has clearly not been watching world events unfold across the decades since the Second World War. America does not have to *try* to become the most powerful and influential state in the world, it unquestionably already *is*. It is not my job to comment on the advisability of such a strategy and it is obvious, even amongst many people living in the United States, that the concept of the new world order is not always acceptable – especially to conservative Christians.

What ought to be mentioned, however, is that we live in what must be the most peaceful times for decades. Detractors would point to the Gulf Wars and to the war in Afghanistan, but though these have been undoubted tragedies for those involved, they are small-scale conflicts in comparison with what took place in the first half of the 20th century.

Terrorism rears its head regularly, but again its results, no matter how well reported and devastating for those touched by such events, are not significant in terms of the level of violence that has marred the history of humanity for countless centuries. It seems as though the world's Inspector General is doing its job, even if a great many people wish it would mind its own business.

But before we move on it might be worth looking at the research of Steven Pinker, a Canadian-American psychologist and writer on scientific subjects. Pinker is definitely of the opinion that we now live in the most peaceful times ever – which might seem absurd, but it's all a matter of scale. There are far more people living in the world today than has ever been the case before. The vast majority, even in comparatively poor countries, live peaceful, productive lives and, again even in poorer countries, average life expectancy is going up. We should not judge this as a reason to stop trying to improve our world, but we do have to be realistic about the past.

Pinker suggests that, in order to know just how violent we are now in comparison with the remote past, we have to look at the way people died, and how young they were when they did. Pinker points to the work of archaeologist Lawrence Keeley, who looked at contemporary hunter-gatherer tribes.

Keeley argued that only by looking at the casualty rates of hunter-gatherers fighting each other could we ascertain what life was truly like for us, back in the days of the 'noble savage'. The results were startling. The chance of dying a violent death, for any person living in the remote past, was anything between 15 per cent and 60 per cent.

Now if we look at the 20th century we discover that the chance of a European or an American man being killed as a result of violence was less than 1 per cent, and that includes the carnage of the First and Second World Wars. It sounds incredible, but it is true.

Pinker comments that, if the death rate amongst tribal hunter-gatherers had prevailed amongst modern humans, the 20th century would have seen

2 billion deaths due to warfare, as opposed to 100 million. If people think there are more murders these days, they should think again. The criminologist Manuel Eisner analysed data from medieval Europe and discovered that, only a few hundred years ago, death by murder accounted for 100 in 100,000, whereas in modern Europe it is less than 1 per 100,000 – a fantastic reduction.

Finally Pinker points out that, across the planet, deaths in individual wars have fallen from 65,000 deaths per conflict to less than 2,000 in the present decade, as well as a 90 per cent decrease in the number of deaths by genocide.

The problem we face these days comes from our very efficient way of reporting news. Once upon a time the average person may only come face to face with a murder in their vicinity once in a lifetime, and perhaps not at all if they lived in a rural community. Now we get everyone's news, no matter where they live, and it all accumulates to make the world seem like a much more violent place than it actually is.

I agree wholeheartedly with Pinker that all of this should not lead us to complacency. There are still far too many violent deaths in the world, but the hopeful part is that they are falling. I estimate that fraternal organizations such as Freemasonry have had a small but important part to play in this. As a historian I know that countless millions of people have died in the name of Christianity, even fighting each other, but wars inspired by Freemasonry are very rare. Even on those occasions when wars such as the American War of Independence might have been influenced by Freemasonic membership, the objective has always been to *free* people and certainly not to enslave them.

We may not have reached the Heaven on Earth that the Star Families have been seeking for centuries but we should at least give ourselves a pat on the back for having made some progress.

At least part of this overall improvement is because of the United States and the tremendous influence it has in the world. It is not a perfect nation by any means but it is a broadly democratic one. It seems we live in extremely cynical times because we all feel that those in power are somehow out to swindle us in every way possible, yet average life-expectancy is increasing, cures are being found for diseases that once killed millions and, as we have seen, fewer people are dying in wars than ever before.

We have a long way to go before we can create a Heaven on Earth, but we may have taken the first faltering steps in that direction.

So we now come to the 10-million-dollar question. It seems certain that *something* of great importance and of significant age was brought to the United States during the Civil War and that it was laid probably with great, if secret, ceremony, in a vault that had been constructed just outside the president's back door.

Before that, this treasure had occupied Rosslyn Chapel in Scotland, and probably also the Cathedral of Chartres in France. It came, originally, from a secret vault under the Temple of Solomon and, before that, it may have been laid in Jerusalem by people who lived so long ago we cannot, in all fairness, attribute to them a religion or a nationhood.

It is this very chamber of secrets that Dan Brown's hero was seeking in his novel *The Lost Symbol* but, at the end, he failed to find it. Brown asserts that the real treasure house was to be found in the hearts of Freemasons, and other people of good conscience. But might this have been nothing more than a red herring, or an admission on Brown's part that he couldn't find what he was looking for?

It is not long since I last stood behind a fence, staring at the very spot that even the Founding Fathers of the United States knew would one day hold something of great worth. In all probability, whatever lies below that turf will only see the light of day when those safeguarding it estimate that the world is ready for the consequences. When we are wise and clever enough to work out what it is, that time may have come.

CHAPTER FOURTEEN

THE SUBTERRANEAN VAULT

What's Hidden in Ellipse Park?

A t the very centre of the Ellipse in Washington DC and just below the turf, there is a small, square marker stone. I accept that this stone exists, though I have not been able to see it for myself. Those who have seen the stone report that it is extremely difficult to find, and this is probably intentional on the part of the Washington authorities.

The more famous Jefferson Stone, which stands 459 metres (1,506ft) south of the Ellipse Meridian Stone, has suffered from the ravages of time and even had to be replaced when it was accidentally dug up during the post-Civil War cleanup of Washington DC. The Ellipse Meridian Stone, deliberately set below the level of the turf, should fare better.

The Ellipse Meridian Stone carries a very simple inscription. It merely says 'Meridian 1890'. Undoubtedly, if we were to ask the authorities what is located beneath the centre of the Ellipse, they would suggest that this small stone, together with a number of sewers that traverse the Ellipse, are all that could be found there. It is true that there are sewers under the Ellipse, and there are iron manhole covers to prove the fact, though as far as we could tell the line of these sewers does not intersect the centre of the Ellipse.

The suggestion that there are tunnels under Washington DC is nothing new. These have been reported for decades and it would be very strange if they did not exist. Through the long, dark days of the Cold War the capital of the United States was under constant threat of nuclear attack from the Eastern Bloc. On one or two occasions the world came close to being involved in nuclear confrontation and it is unthinkable that the administrative and military authorities in Washington DC were not somehow protected in case of such an eventuality. Such a strike could have come at very short notice, making it difficult to get the president and his associates out of the city quickly enough. Many people report that such tunnels do exist and that there are tunnels connecting the White House to other important buildings up and down the Mall, and probably also to the Capitol. Like many commentators, rather than being surprised if such tunnels turned out to be a reality, I would be astounded if they were not.

It is not even out of the question that the vault below the centre of the Ellipse, directly under the Ellipse Meridian Stone, is connected to a known tunnel system designed so that the infrastructure of Washington DC could go on running in case of a nuclear strike, though it is much more likely that the Ellipse vault stands alone and is accessible only from ground level at the centre of the Ellipse. In all probability its entrance is some feet below the ground, back-filled and with only the small marker stone above it betraying its position.

Those who originally engineered the Ellipse vault were clearly following Freemasonic tradition and legend, so these stories might give us a clue what the vault looks like. For a description we need to turn to Scottish Rite Freemasonry, which describes the chamber originally created on Mount Moriah by Enoch. Ultimately, this would also be the spot where the Jerusalem Temple was located, but Enoch dates so far back that the Hebrews did not even exist as a nation at the time.

Freemasonic legend tells us that Enoch's chamber was composed of nine brick vaults. These were placed one on top of another, with access via a portal in the arched roof of each vault. If the chamber under the Ellipse is a copy of Enoch's original chamber in Jerusalem, it need not take up much space in terms of area, but it would be very deep. This would seem to conform to the reports of Lieutenant Colonel Thomas Lincoln Casey in 1878 that only the very centre of the Ellipse was inaccessible to him and his men.

At an earlier stage, such a deep chamber might have presented problems in the topography of Washington DC, but it seems most likely that the chamber was indeed created in the years leading up to 1880. By this time Portland cement, for the making of concrete, was in use and had been so for four decades or more. Using concrete, the chamber could have been 'tanked' or lined in such a way that groundwater was excluded from the chamber which, in theory, could be as dry today as it was when finished in the late 19th century.

It is also possible that the chamber under the Ellipse is nothing like as elaborate as the description of Enoch's vaults. Had it been so, it seems unlikely that no mention of it emerged at the time because it would have taken a great many workers to create it. If, on the other hand, those taking part genuinely did think they were co-operating in the construction of sewer chambers, the whole project would have attracted little attention or comment and only a select few would have known its real purpose.

On balance, it seems most likely that what lies below the Ellipse is a fairly simple, possibly arched chamber, deep enough not to be disturbed by any remedial work necessary at the surface of the Ellipse, and probably only large enough to contain whatever was intended to be placed there in the 19th century. Such a project would have been easy to address with 19th-century technology and without raising undue suspicion from people such as Lieutenant Colonel Casey (who in any case could easily have been kept quiet on the grounds of supposed national security).

Once the vault was completed and the artefacts carefully wrapped and protected, they could have been committed to the chamber, which would then have been sealed and the entrance backfilled. In all probability the chamber has never been disturbed since, and will not be opened until those responsible for its protection consider the world is ready for what the chamber's contents will reveal.

In order to ascertain what the Ellipse Chamber does contain, we need to look once again at Masonic tradition. This takes us back to that enigmatic character Enoch who, although mentioned very little in the surviving Old Testament, was once a pivotal character and of the greatest significance. Because the Book of Enoch demonstrates that he visited the site of Newgrange in Ireland at a time when it was still functioning, we can be sure that Enoch is dateable to a period sometime around or before 3000 BC.

King Solomon did not build his Temple in Jerusalem until about 960 BC, which means that the stories of Enoch were already ancient by the time of Solomon. Enoch lived in the Neolithic period, when the ideas of a patriarchal monotheistic deity, such as that embraced by the Hebrews, did not even exist, and at a time when the Great Goddess reigned supreme across Europe and far beyond.

Religious imperatives change from age to age, though specific characters from history and prehistory remain and often tend to be modified in the light of whatever social and religious norm prevails at the time. As a result, it seems extremely likely that the Hebrews could have seen Enoch as part of their own culture. After such a protracted period the details surrounding the character would have become blurred and they doubtless assumed that Enoch had venerated the very same Storm God Jehovah that they embraced. The fact that Enoch's beliefs might have been significantly different would be unknown.

What we do know about Enoch is that he brought knowledge to the people of his time. In Hebrew his name is *Sol Henoch*, which means 'to initiate' or 'to instruct'. Masonic tradition asserts that Enoch was given 30 volumes by God, which contained all the existing knowledge and information about secret sciences. Enoch was also known to the Babylonians, who ascribed to him the birth of the study of astronomy, which again links him to the Neolithic period and the observatories of the Megalithic people of Britain and Ireland.

Before we look at Enoch's other famous treasure, it is worth mentioning that Mount Moriah, where Jerusalem was eventually located, has always had a strong connection with the planet Venus and with the deity that bears the same name. The name 'Jerusalem' actually means 'place of the rising Venus' and, long after the Temple was finally destroyed, the Romans built another temple dedicated to Venus very close by. This was ultimately destroyed by the Emperor Constantine who built the Church of the Holy Sepulchre on the site, which is said to mark the spot where Jesus was buried.

This connects Mount Moriah with Rosslyn Chapel where Venus was watched from the observatory platform and where its light was recreated in the form of the Shekinah over the great east window. And there is a direct connection with Washington DC which, as we have seen, was created with Venus and the zodiac sign of Virgo in mind.

Another popular assertion from Scottish Rite Freemasonry is that Enoch had created a golden triangle – otherwise referred to as a 'chevron'. Each of the sides of the triangle was 1 cubit in length. This golden plate was covered with precious stones and, emblazoned upon it, was the true name of the Deity. This, Enoch put upon a white, cylindrical marble pillar to be placed in the lowest and therefore the most inaccessible of his nine chambers.

Because Enoch knew that a great flood was coming, he also created two columns, one of marble and one of brass. Upon the pillar of brass he engraved the history of creation and a description of all the arts and sciences he understood, together with information regarding the speculative freemasonry of his day. On the marble pillar he left instructions as to the place of the subterranean vault. He used marble so that the pillar could withstand fire, and brass to survive the deluge that was to come.

For their book *Uriel's Machine*, Christopher Knight and Robert Lomas looked in detail at the stories of Enoch, as well as examining whether something akin to the Flood of the biblical stories had ever really taken place. Their conclusions were stunning. They put the stories of the Flood down to a genuine natural disaster that took place in the remote past, in 7640 BC. Their suggestion is that, prior to this event, caused by a collision of a meteorite or a cometary fragment with the Earth, a previous, now lost civilization that existed on our planet was almost completely destroyed.

The theory is that the astronomers of this lost culture were quite aware that the disaster was going to take place, taking specific steps to ensure that at least something of their culture and vast knowledge would survive. One of their number, Uriel, was the person who instructed Enoch and ensured, through him, that important aspects of the civilization would be safeguarded. It was this information that composed the 30 volumes and which formed the hieroglyphic writing on the two pillars.

This research by Knight and Lomas had little or nothing to do with our common effort to understand the Megalithic Yard or our findings with regard to the greater Megalithic system as a whole. However, we were forced back down this track in researching our book *Civilization One* because of our ultimate conclusions regarding the Megalithic system.

True, we had established that the Megalithic Yard was easy enough to reproduce if one knew the simple instructions for doing so, but it formed only one part of a cohesive whole that measured distance, time, volume and mass (*see* Appendix One). The whole system was based around the mass of the Earth and it took into account the physical dimensions not only of the Earth but also of the Moon and the Sun. It seemed impossible to us that some of the information inherent in the system could possibly have been available to naked-eye astronomers of the Megalithic period.

It appeared that *someone* put together the Megalithic system in such a way that it was deliberately engineered to allow an easy recreation of its fundamental linear unit, the Megalithic Yard. But whoever used the Megalithic Yard, and could reproduce it, did not need to have full knowledge of the entire system. If the plain and simple facts had been bestowed upon a special 'priest class', deliberately created by Uriel and his kind, the reality of the Megalithic Yard could bridge the impending disaster because, although the majority of people would die, some would survive.

These people did not need to know a great deal. If they were instilled with the importance of the Megalithic Yard, probably in a religious sense, they would keep on using it – even though they had little or no idea of its ultimate genius or the implications it had regarding the knowledge of those who taught it.

Once Chris and I learned to understand the Megalithic system, we turned our eyes outward and discovered how relevant it was to the Moon and Sun. We also took note of how its basic unit of mass, the pound, fitted so accurately but completely unexpectedly into the mass of the Earth. The more we learned, the greater was our respect for whoever had created the system because, in a holistic sense, it is a clear improvement on the measuring systems we use today, even the metric system. In the present age we have never allied the measurement of time to the metric system, whereas with the Megalithic system time measurement is an integral part of the whole.

In short, it became obvious to us that the Megalithic people of Europe had not created the Megalithic system of measurement – they simply did not possess the necessary tools to do so. How could they possibly have known the circumference of the Earth, not to mention those of other planetary bodies? How would it have been possible for them to ascertain the mass of the Earth, which has been known only for a comparatively short period of time in our present age? The plain, unvarnished truth had to be that, as bright as Megalithic astronomers were, when it came to the overall genius of the Megalithic system, they were clearly very much in the dark. They were simply doing what they had been taught to do – most likely in the guise of a religious imperative.

Like Alexander Thom had done with the Megalithic monuments, we had 'back-engineered' the Megalithic system, thanks to the existence of the Megalithic Yard, the Minoan Foot, the number patterns used on the Phaistos Disc and a few surviving units in the pre-metric system of measurements. The fact that we were able to do so was due in great measure to modern technology, such as computers and scientific calculators.

Someone had managed to create a uniform, totally integrated system of measures and weights that was drawn directly from the reality of the Earth and parts of our solar system. The real genius lay in the fact that they had created such a fantastic system, without ever having to split a number into fractions or decimals – the whole thing relies on integers.

It is self-evident that the teaching of the basic principles of the Megalithic Yard, probably to many hundreds of people, was a 'second line' strategy on behalf of the 'Watchers' (the name given to these people by Enoch and used by Knight and Lomas). It was done, probably at comparatively short notice, in the hope that, if the overall history and accomplishments of the earlier civilization did not prevail, at least something of their genius would survive so that someone in the distant future could extrapolate the bigger story from it. That is exactly what Chris Knight and I have been able to do.

All the same, it looks as though much more information regarding the Watchers did survive, against all odds, buried in the deep chamber that Enoch and his companions created on Mount Moriah. It is quite likely that Enoch never fully understood the total implications of the information he was handling, even though he was obviously a competent astronomer and had been carefully schooled by the Watchers.

Freemasonic stories suggest that the writing on the two pillars was in a form of hieroglyphics, and it is quite likely that the writing in the 30 volumes given to Enoch was the same. Future generations would not have understood what was being communicated. After all, even Egyptian hieroglyphics were not understood until the early 19th century and the hieroglyphics used by the Minoans on Crete still have not been deciphered.

To those who saw the volumes throughout much of history, this would have been the handwriting of God. They knew it was important because legend told them it was so. But it had not come from God. Rather it was the accumulated science and wisdom of a civilization virtually wiped out by a natural disaster.

This then is the information that slept away several thousand years under Mount Moriah, before it was found by King Solomon's engineers. It was then reburied and stayed below the Temple of Jerusalem until once again unearthed by the first Knights Templar. Clearly, an understanding of the whereabouts of the cache had been passed down through the Star Families, but it could not be recovered until Jerusalem was in friendly hands long enough for the excavation to be made.

The brightest of those amongst the First Crusaders that took and held Jerusalem must have known in their hearts that their stay in the region could only be temporary. Clearly the treasure of Enoch had to be removed and taken somewhere safe, until the time came for it to be seen by society as a whole. It was most likely taken initially to Chartres, in France, or Troyes in Champagne.

But when the Knights Templar were threatened, they removed the treasure to Scotland, where it ultimately found a custom-built repository at Rosslyn Chapel. But even this turned out to be temporary. If the documents were ever to be opened, and if the world was ever going to benefit from the information they contained, it needed to be in a re-creation of the Utopian ideal that Jerusalem had represented. It had to be in a 'New Jerusalem'.

By this time much of the Star Family interest was vested in Freemasonry, an organization specifically created to preserve the most ancient of religions and to safeguard the secrets that most Freemasons don't even know exist.

It may be the case that present society has caught up with the Watchers in terms of our scientific knowledge and understanding, but on the other hand they may still have plenty to teach us about the cosmos and its workings. What the hidden documents of Enoch could certainly tell us is exactly where we came from, and what our earthly legacy was before the disaster that took place so long ago.

In some way that we will probably never know until the documents are seen and deciphered, there is an association between the Earth and the planet Venus that surpasses our present understanding. It is also clear that the feminine-based religion that predominated in Megalithic times, and which was superseded only a few thousand years ago, was indeed the belief of the Watchers and their society. It has been perpetuated for countless centuries by the Star Families and was expressed all over Washington DC – the New Jerusalem.

The Megalithic Yard and at least some aspects of Megalithic geometry were remembered in very specific circles, and they were used in the underlying construction of Washington DC. Indeed we can say for certain that someone in a position of high authority there recognizes them to this day.

As to the nature of the 30 volumes that I am convinced are sleeping below the Ellipse in Washington DC, we can be fairly sure that they are not books in the modern sense of the word. It is more likely that they would be scrolls, though we could hardly expect papyrus or parchment scrolls to have survived for such a long period.

They are more likely to be made of metal and, since gold is the most resilient and unchanging of metals, it is most likely that Enoch's scrolls are composed of very thin, beaten gold, upon which the hieroglyphs were either engraved or stamped.

Such metal scrolls are not without parallel. Amongst the Dead Sea Scrolls found in the Jordan Valley in the 1940s was one made of copper, though even copper is unlikely to have lasted for upwards of 10,000 years. Gold, on the other hand, could last almost indefinitely. It does not corrode and changes of temperature or humidity have little bearing on it. If the 30 scrolls had been carefully wrapped and handled with reverence on the few occasions they have seen the light of day, they could be almost as perfect now as they were when Enoch first placed them in his chamber.

As to the two pillars, of brass and marble, these surely did not survive because the legends assert that they were outside the chamber and that they carried information as to where the chamber was located.

From the moment surviving Star Family members chose to build their New Jerusalem on the banks of the Potomac, laying out their plans for the city on paper, that huge Megalithic arrow has been pointing to the very spot where the treasure of Enoch was to be located.

Perhaps other treasures from below the original Temple are also to be found under the Ellipse, though it is unlikely that any of them could be of greater interest or more use to humanity than the scrolls containing so much information about our remote past.

I cannot begin to guess what the trigger will be for these treasures to be brought to light. The Star Families have always kept one step ahead of the game regarding the cache and, if they suspect that society is not yet ready for the information they safeguard, and yet its location becomes seriously suspected, they would be likely to remove the scrolls to some other location.

On the other hand, Washington DC fits the bill more than any other location where the scrolls have been kept since they were first committed to the earth. The orientation of Washington DC and the District of Columbia was created with this priceless treasure in mind. Meanwhile, the United States is the Inspector General of the world. The proliferation of English across the planet provides us with the best lingua franca that has existed since the Tower of Babel and, whether we like it or not, the world is growing smaller, gradually becoming *one society*. The process is slow and creaky, and there is still much hostility and bloodshed in the world but, as we have seen, our planet has never been as peaceful as it is right now – no matter what we might instinctively think to the contrary.

When Chris Knight and I took a walk along the Mall in Washington DC for the first time after the information about its Megalithic credentials came to light, I looked at the city in an entirely different way. I was able to open my eyes and to see things that had been 'hidden in plain sight' for so long.

I saw the east–west alignment of the Mall, and the huge statue of the Goddess on the Capitol dome, looking east towards each new dawn. I could see how the sign of Virgo would rise above the statue late in September and then roll across the sky to the south before turning north again, being pierced by the tall shaft of the Washington Monument.

I stood on the line of the intended prime meridian and stared both north and south, in the direction of the intersections of the Columbia diamond, and I could see that this same line passed right through the middle of the White House, across the very centre of the Ellipse and also through the Jefferson Monument. As we walked around the city over a number of days I was stunned by the sheer number of representations of the Goddess to be seen at almost every intersection and circle, and at the incidence of statuary and artwork that displays representations of the sign of Virgo.

I was able to stand by the Pentagon, a concrete essence of the 32nd degree of Scottish Rite Freemasonry, and I took note of that 33 Megalithic Second triangle that put the seal on the importance of this place. Surely, I told myself, if the United States had failed to respond to what was happening in Europe in 1940, Hitler's boast of a thousand-year Reich may well have come to pass and the world would have entered another sinister dark age.

Staring north, I wondered if successive presidents who have worked at their desk in the Oval Office of the White House had any comprehension of what was really taking place around them. At least some of them did.

But my longest and hardest stare was from behind a fence at that truly awe-inspiring spot, right at the centre of the Ellipse. I could see it clearly and I knew that, even standing where I was, in all probability I was directly above the chamber where I believe those solid gold scrolls are sleeping.

I only hope that the 'Providence' of which Thomas Jefferson and others were so fond grants me sufficient time to be able to view those incredible documents at first hand. Somehow I doubt it, but like the amazing species of which I am a member, I deal in reality but live in hope.

THE MEGALITHIC SYSTEM

This Appendix first appeared in *Before the Pyramids*, written by Christopher Knight and myself. I include it here with the permission of Chris Knight and for the benefit of readers who wish to better understand what the Megalithic system of measurements is about.

Long before telescopes were invented, human beings already showed an interest in astronomy. We are, by nature, an inquisitive species and we want to know what makes everything work, so this interest in the sky isn't all that surprising. In addition to simple curiosity it was probably also important to understand the workings of the sky for another reason. The sky was where the gods lived, so understanding its workings and cycles probably seemed to bring one closer to understanding the minds of the gods.

There were also very practical reasons for understanding the patterns and movements of heavenly objects. The Sun, Moon and planets keep their own cycles, some of which are very important to farming communities and to cultures that rely on hunting, especially if migratory species are involved. With a good understanding of the patterns formed by the Sun it is possible to measure the year and to make note of what should be done and when.

It seems to have been a very long time ago when it occurred to someone that the replicating patterns of the day and night fitted a certain number of times into the replicating patterns of the year. They didn't need to know that the Earth spins on its own axis or that it travels around the Sun. All they had to do was to watch what happened over their heads and to be able to measure and memorize the patterns involved.

Working out the number of days in a year wouldn't have been all that easy using the Sun. This is because it is so bright and because of its movements along the eastern horizon throughout the year. As the Sun gets to its extremes of north and south it slows down significantly and, for some days, it appears to rise in almost exactly the same place, so which of these sunrises marks the end of one year and the beginning of another?

Stars are more obliging and will pop up in the same place on the horizon night after night. The only time they can't be seen is when the Sun is in the same part of the sky for two or three months.

To accurately measure the length of a year both the Sun and stars were needed. Super-henges, such as the Thornborough Henge complex, were built with this need partly in mind. In the case of Thornborough, the gap in the henges to the southeast was deliberately placed very close to where the star Sirius rose each night, and also where the Sun also rose at the time of its most southerly rising (the winter solstice).

It is a consequence of the Earth travelling around the Sun and maintaining a particular angle relative to the Sun that makes the Sun appear to rise and set on different parts of the horizon throughout the year. In the northern hemisphere the Sun rises well north of east in summer and well south of east during the winter months. When seen from Thornborough around 3500 BC it never travelled any further south than the southeastern henge entrances and this was the position it achieved on the day of the midwinter solstice (the shortest day).

Those keeping observations at Thornborough knew full well that by the time the Sun travelled north from its rising in the southeastern gaps, and then returned again, Sirius would have risen in the same gap 366 times. This told them there were 366 days in a year. This is a star year and is not the same as a solar year.

As far as the observer is concerned it amounts to this. A solar year is just over 365.25 days in length but during the same time a star will have risen 366 times. Each day, according to the rising of a star (a sidereal day), is 23 hours 56 minutes 4 seconds in length, whereas an average solar day is 24 hours in length. That leaves a discrepancy of 236 seconds which, over a year, amounts to almost exactly 24 hours. It is part of the clockwork mechanism of our solar system that there are different sorts of years, dependent on what one is observing. Our Megalithic and pre-Megalithic ancestors in Britain focused on the number of times a star rose in a year, and the result was 366 times.

Having made this realization, what they did next is the most surprising aspect of our studies across the last two decades. They created an integrated measuring system based upon a year of 366 days. Just as surely as they recognized the year could be split into 366 units, they also split the sky into 366 units, which we would know as degrees of arc. They then split the units again, first into minutes of arc. They considered that there were 60 minutes of arc to 1 degree of arc.

But this wasn't enough for them so they split the units again. Each minute of arc was split into six smaller units, which we would know as seconds of arc. Note the difference between this form of geometry and the one we use now: in 360° geometry there are 60 seconds of arc to 1 minute of arc but in the Megalithic system there are only 6.

Somehow they worked out that if they split the degree, minute and second of arc in this way they would arrive at a stunning result. They reasoned that if the sky was a great circle, the size and shape of the Earth must be the same circle turned inside out. In other words, if they could split the sky into 366 units, they could split the surface of the Earth in the same way. When they did this the Megalithic Second of arc of the polar Earth measured *exactly* 366MY.

The actual size of the Megalithic Yard could be judged by the careful use of a pendulum of exactly half this length. At first this was used in conjunction with the Sun but later a more sophisticated method was established using the planet Venus during certain parts of its orbit.

What is absolutely incredible about the Megalithic Yard (82.966cm) as a unit of length is not just that it is geodetic (it fits into the polar circumference of the Earth in a logical and obviously intended way), but it does the same job on the Moon and the Sun. One Megalithic Second of arc on the Moon measures exactly 100MY. On the Sun the same Megalithic Second of arc is 40,000MY.

Getting the sheer genius of this system across to our readers has been the hardest part of our quest because it really is incredible, but it can seem complicated. Once the penny drops, the whole system is virtually miraculous. In this system, a second of arc of the sky can be seen as the same thing as a second of time of the Earth turning on its axis. In other words, 1 Megalithic Second of the Earth turning on its axis also represents a physical segment of the sky, albeit an extremely small one, because it is 1×366th of 1×360th of the sky. The same second is also a finite measurement of part of the Earth's circumference. Time and geometry and distance all merge into the same symmetrical whole and astronomical calculations become much easier.

Meanwhile, with the system we use today we have degrees, minutes and seconds of arc of the sky and of the circumference of our planet. We also have minutes and seconds of time but these don't match the turning sky at all. This must have cost thousands of human lives as the first mariners to engage in transatlantic voyages tried desperately to reconcile minutes and seconds of time with minutes and seconds of geometrical arc, coming up with the wrong answer.

We eventually discovered that, in addition to measuring time and linear distance, the Megalithic system had also been based on the mass of the Earth. How could this possibly be? The unit of mass in question is virtually the same as the unit presently known as the imperial pound. The mass of the Earth is 5.9742×10^{24} kilograms. In pounds this figure is $1.31708565 \times 10^{25}$ pounds. With just a very slight change in the definition of the pound, this figure becomes 1.317600×10^{25} pounds and then something amazing happens. Imagine we segment the Earth like an orange. A segment one Megalithic Second of arc across would have a mass of exactly 1×10^{20} pounds. That's 10,000,000,000,000,000,000 pounds!

This means that the imperial pound (lb) and the pound that was a part of the Megalithic system are virtually identical. The Megalithic pound had a value of 99.96 per cent of the modern pound! The difference is 0.4 of a gram. That this level of accuracy has been maintained across such a vast period of time is little short of incredible.

In order to turn the Megalithic Yard into a system for measuring volume and mass we need to resort to the Megalithic Inch. Alexander Thom found this unit when he carefully studied carvings that had been scratched into a number of standing stones. He established that there had been 40 Megalithic Inches to 1 Megalithic Yard. A cube with sides of 1/10th of a Megalithic Yard (4 Megalithic Inches) has the same volume as a modern pint of water. If the water is poured out and the same cube is filled with any cereal grain, such as wheat, barley or even un-hulled rice, the weight of the cereal grain will be 1 pound.

So what do we have?

The Megalithic system is a system of geometry and measurement that is based upon a 366-day year, together with the physical size and mass of the Earth. It measures time, distance, mass and volume using the same figures throughout. Aspects of it are as relevant to the Moon and Sun as they are here on Earth. Without wishing to detract from our stunning scientific accomplishments as a species, anyone would surely have to admit that the Megalithic system is better in a number of ways than any method of measurement used today: it is *integrated* and a common terminology is used throughout. The metric system in use today may be extremely accurate, and it too was originally based on the circumference of the Earth, but it certainly does not take Earth mass into account and neither is it used for the measurement of time.

Unbelievable as it may seem, thanks to our friend and colleague Edmund Sixsmith we now believe that the Megalithic system also dealt with the measurement of temperature. If we create a temperature scale in which the freezing point of water is 0° Megalithic and the boiling point of water is 366° Megalithic, something quite magical happens. Absolute zero, the lowest temperature achievable (usually considered to be -273.15°C) becomes a totally round and quite accurate temperature, -1,000° Megalithic.

Since there is little chance that our Megalithic ancestors were interested in measuring temperatures, let alone being in possession of the technology to do so, the Megalithic temperature system stands as proof that, ingenious and useable as aspects of the Megalithic system were to our ancient ancestors, they did not create it. Rather they must have *inherited* it from a previous technological culture that is now lost to us.

THE SUMERIAN
SYSTEM

It was with the greatest surprise that we (Christopher Knight and myself) discovered that the metric system of measurement, which is supposed to have been created in late-18th-century France, was already ancient and that it had been used thousands of years earlier by the early inhabitants of Mesopotamia, the Sumerians.

In Chapter 9 of this book I dealt with a new and revolutionary measuring system proposed by American statesman and president Thomas Jefferson. I indicated that Jefferson's suggested measuring systems were independent of the metric system, but Jefferson, a scientist in his own right, had visited France for a number of years just prior to the adoption of the metric system. Not only would he have fully understood it, but he may also have had a hand in designing it. This book explains why Jefferson decided that his own system of measurements was better than the proposed metric system, though the United States did not adopt his suggestions.

What those who created the metric system may or may not have known was that almost everything they were striving to achieve had been done before – almost 4,000 years before! The acceptance that the metric system of measurement, as advanced as its creators believed it to be, had been equalled and probably bettered so long ago, would come as a great embarrassment to science. This was pointed out before Christopher Knight and I published anything on the subject, but through an ingenious range of obfuscations and a point-blank refusal to accept irrefutable evidence, those responsible have made certain the world remains ignorant.

Readers who are interested to go beyond the observations I have made regarding the metric system and that created by the Sumerians may be interested by what lies below. It is an explanation of the Sumerian system, also pointing out how and why modern experts refuse to accept the ingenuity of this ancient system. This appendix also explains that the Sumerian system, just like the Megalithic system, was based on the beat and length of a specific pendulum – though in the case of the Sumerian system there was also another way of verifying the basic linear unit (which was basically the same as a metre), using nothing more sophisticated than barley seeds.

Introduction

We contend that the Sumerians had a fully integrated measuring system superior in some ways to the one we presently use. This statement is not made lightly; neither do we belittle the efforts of the scientific community during the last couple of centuries to build a range of universally accepted measurements that are more accurate than any that went before. The reason we suggest the Sumerian system is in some ways superior lies in the fact that to the Sumerians the measurement of time and the methodology of geometry were part of an integrated whole. This is not the case with the metric system, because the way we measure geometry and time is still essentially Sumerian, with a sexagesimal base. We further contend that all the basic elements of the metric system existed in the Sumerian model.

It seems likely that the system in its entirety existed from a very early period. Ultimately in Mesopotamia there was a confusing array of weights and measures. However, the linear length that was the 'kush' or 'barley cubit', the volume unit known as the 'sila' and the weight unit called the 'mana' remained generally consistent throughout Sumerian times. In the case of the kush we have statues carefully defining what its length was intended to be. There are many examples of the mana, with a variation in size itemized below, and a couple of examples of the sila, which also broadly conform to our discoveries.

We do not contend that across the whole of Mesopotamian civilization every unit of length, mass and volume used remained faithful to the model we show below. Even from Britain's own fairly immediate past, there is a distinct lack of conformity in weights and measures, though a broad *intention* can still be discerned.

The tools we have used to reconstruct the system in its entirety come from a number of different sources. The measurement of time and geometry are still with us today and appear to be little altered from Sumerian-Babylonian times. We now have 24 hours in a day, which from a mathematical point of view is at odds with the original conception. Twelve hours was undoubtedly the starting point.

The model of Sumerian weights and measures comes direct from archaeological finds and written Sumerian evidence. The ability to put all this together is really a matter of commonsense, experience and direct experimentation. As one example, instead of assuming the Sumerians used a hypothetical barley seed as a basis for their length and mass units, we measured and weighed barley seeds, which experts don't seem to have done.

It is worth mentioning at this point the well-attested habit of the Sumerians to use half and double units, which seem to have been interchangeable. In our opinion, with time, some of the original units became better known in their half or double forms. It is also possible that inscriptions from the period have been misunderstood. A good example of this would be the kush or barley cubit. Its usual form was 49.94cm in length but this form was equal to only 180 barley seeds, divided into 30 units known as fingers. We believe that at the origin of the system the double-kush was quite clearly used. It is comprised of 360 barley seeds, divided into 60 fingers. Our own evidence shows *why* the double-kush is the logical starting point, but this is confirmed to a great extent by common logic. The Sumerians were obsessed with the numbers 60 and 360, which appear throughout their system of mathematics and geometry.

We do not claim to know everything about the Sumerian system, and it is possible that some of the half or double units favoured at different times were adopted for sound mathematical reasons. Once again we might look at time measurement. We know that the Sumerians used both 12-hour and 24-hour days, but we don't pretend to understand why.

Our finished model works perfectly and every part of it is taken directly from historical or archaeological evidence where it is available. We have merely filled in the gaps, which we see as being a valid exercise. If a palaeontologist discovers parts of the fossilized skull of a particular sort of dinosaur that hasn't been found before, he can reconstruct it even though he hasn't seen the creature in question. Why? Because there are certain things about skulls that remain constant, no matter what the species. The same is true with mathematical patterns and especially those of the Sumerians. We have done no more than the palaeontologist. If the finished picture is surprising or even astounding, that does not mean the picture is wrong; it simply suggests our previous understanding of the culture in question was lacking.

Geometry and the Year

Our destination is an understanding of what turns out to be a deeply integrated and holistic measuring system. For this reason it is somewhat difficult to know where to enter it or to establish what came first. It seems sensible to start with geometry because this was an expression of everything else. At school, many of us were taught that geometry was a Greek invention. This isn't the case because both the Sumerians and the Egyptians were using geometry before the rise of the ancient Greeks.

On a balance of probabilities, there is little doubt that geometry was first used by the Sumerians. Geometry follows the same sexagesimal pattern that exists throughout all Sumerian mathematics and it almost certainly started out as part of a method of measuring time. Nobody doubts that the Sumerians invented the form of time measurement we still use today and we hope to show that geometry was merely a variant of time measurement.

It is most likely that geometry began as an expression of the year. To understand how this might be, we must first look at what appears to have been the very first way of subdividing a year in the Near and Middle East. Ancient people were responsive above all to two celestial bodies, the Sun and Moon. Both heavenly bodies, when seen from Earth, seem to travel in a great circle across the sky. The band of space through which they travel is known as the 'plane of the ecliptic'. From a very early period the backdrop of stars along the ecliptic was divided into 12 sections. Why was this the case? Almost certainly because, whilst the Sun took a year to go round the whole circle of the heavens, the Moon travelled the distance much more quickly. In every year the Moon made 12 journeys around the heavens whilst the Sun made only 1. Each full moon would occur $\frac{1}{12}$ of the great circle of heaven further on than the previous full moon. It may have been an attempt to track the patterns of the Moon within the solar year that led to the subdivision of the ecliptic. These divisions are known to us as the signs of the zodiac.

We know for sure that the Moon's orbit was the origin of modern months, not least of all because the word 'month' derives from the name of the Moon. We also know that the Sumerians did use lunar months. These were 'synodic' months. The synodic lunar month is that period between one full moon and the next, and it takes 29.53 days.

Twelve months of 29.53 days does not correspond with the true length of a year – it is nearly 11 days short. The Sumerians didn't really worry about that. They simply added an extra month to the calendar now and again when necessary. However, 12 lunar periods equalled 354 days, which must have proved hopeless from a mathematical point of view. The Sumerian priests seem to have decided that the best way to deal with the situation was to consider every period from one full moon to the next to be 30 days in length and to have a 'Priest's Year' of 360 days. However, the original lunar month, which commenced with the first sighting of the new moon, also continued to be used for other purposes.

The 30-day month and the 360-day year developed early in Sumerian history. Of course, even 360 days doesn't correspond with the real year, but compensations could be made when necessary. A 12-month, 360-day year provides a good model for subdividing the day, which is what happened.

Dividing the Day

Surviving documents indicate that the most usual way for the Sumerians to split the day was into 12 units, known to us as hours. There are examples of a 24-hour split, because each of the 12 hours was sometimes referred to as 'double hours'. However, it can be seen right across Mesopotamian mathematics that different patterns fit each other like Russian dolls. It can be observed that the splitting of the day is a microcosm of the splitting of the year, about which there is no doubt.

The hours of the day were, in a practical sense, not of equal length. It depended on the time of year and the daylight available. However, it is obvious throughout Sumerian metrology that what happened in the real world and what took place in the ordered mind of the priests and scribes were two different things. In any case, hours would average out in the end. What was just as important as the hours was the 'gesh'. We know for a fact that by the third millennium BC the Sumerians were dividing the day into 360 units, each known as 'gesh'. This became very important to our research. Much of what has been published about Sumerian timekeeping, and substantiated by his reproduction of texts, we owe to Samuel Noah Kramer, one of the most acclaimed Sumerologists.

Kramer was in no doubt that from the scripts the 360-day year and the 360-gesh day were Sumerian inventions.

Minutes and Seconds

There is no definitive proof from Sumerian texts found up until now that the Sumerians invented seconds and minutes of time. It is known that the Babylonians knew about them, and the Babylonians followed the Sumerians. However, we believe we can prove that the second of time existed because it was an intrinsic part of the Sumerian measuring system. The lack of documentary evidence might merely imply that the right document has not yet been found, and should in no way be taken as proof that the second and minute were Babylonian inventions.

As Above, so Below

As with many ancient peoples it appears that the Sumerians thought of the universe in a sort of *telescopic* fashion. Documentary sources show that they divided the year in the same way they divided the day. In other words, 1 day was ⅟₃₆₀ of the ritual year. The number 360 and its multiples occur time and again in the Sumerian system. The Sumerians believed that their progenitor gods had come from a planet or place called Nibir. On this world, they suggested, time passed at a different rate. They thought that every time-increment on the Earth was increased by 3,600 times on Nibir. The fact that we discover that there are 60×60 seconds in an hour, or 3,600 seconds, is therefore no surprise. It merely adds to the Russian doll feel of Sumerian mathematics. This is particularly well highlighted when the priest's month of 30 days is analysed.

The Priest's Month

As we have seen, it is known that the Sumerians used two different sorts of month. These were the true synodic lunar month, the period from just after one new moon to just after the next. This was 29.5 days in length. But they also used a 30-day month, doubtless invented by the priests because it was much tidier. It is our firm belief that in the 30-day month we can locate the origin of modern timekeeping.

If there were 12 hours in a day, then in 30 days there must be 360 hours. This matched the 360 days in the year, so again we can see this as a microcosm in which 1 hour was corresponding to 1 day as a proportion. Each hour was subdivided into 3,600 smaller units, equivalent to a second (though this was twice the length of our second of time because of the 12-hour day).

It can be seen from this that timekeeping was essentially a lunar rather than a solar matter, and that a second of time was the time taken for a second of arc in the movement of a slightly hypothetical 30-day lunar cycle.

Time measurement in the system is as follows:

The Year   = 360 days

The Month   = 30 days

The Day   = 12 hours (each hour is 1° of arc of a 30-day circle)

The Hour   = 60 minutes (each minute is 1 minute of arc of a
                30 day circle)

The minute = 60 seconds (each second is 1 second of arc of a
                30-day circle)

Small increments of time such as the minute and even the second almost certainly did exist in this system, even if the people concerned could not directly measure them. They are inferred from the 30-day month as geometric fractions of that month. However, there is good reason to believe that the second of time was much more than a hypothetical unit to the Sumerians.

The Basic Unit of Length – the Kush

Across the broad span of Mesopotamian history there must have been many different units of linear measurement but there is no doubt that one in particular perpetuated and was used on a regular basis, from very early times. This was the kush or barley cubit. Most agencies agree that the kush was around half a metre in length, but as to its true size, there are examples available. Statues of the Sumerian ruler Gudea, dating from 2125–10 BC, show representations of a half-kush, carefully executed and graduated. These measures exist on two statues and agree closely with each other. From the half-kush on the statues we can infer an intended length for the kush of around 49.94cm. The kush is mentioned regularly in documents from the Sumerian period. It was often used in its half or its double form.

We maintain that the double-kush of 99.88cm was the original measure and that the kush as it became known was simply preferred for the sake of linear convenience.

The Sumerians defined the kush as being equal to 30 shu-si or fingers, each of which contained 6 barley seeds. Bearing in mind the virtual obsession the Sumerians had for the numbers 6 and 360, it seems likely that the original unit devised was what we would now call the double-kush, which would contain 60 shu-si, each containing 6 barley seeds. Thus the total number of barley seeds would be 360. We will show other reasons for believing that the double-kush was the original intended standard unit of length. Judging by the Gudea statues, each calculated double-kush would be 99.88cm in length.

The basic unit of measurement used by the Sumerians, both in terms of length and weight, was the *se* or barley seed. Modern Sumerian experts believe that the barley seed became nothing more than a hypothetical standard – the word *se*, although clearly meaning barley seed, was recognized as a specific measure and became detached from its origins. Although this contention is understandable in terms of what happened to British and French units, which were also originally based on barley and wheat seeds, our investigations reveal that an average barley seed does exactly what the Sumerians suggest, both in terms of linear size and weight.

Metrologists have dismissed the Sumerian assertion that the double-kush was equal to 360 barley seeds, probably because, at some time in the past, experiments were carried out with barley seeds that seemed to lead to the conclusion that the barley seeds would not fit the expected pattern. It is most likely that those carrying out the experiments fully expected that the Sumerians would have laid the barley seeds end to end, as was originally the case with old English and French measurements. However, if the seeds are laid on their sides, front to back, even modern barley seeds almost exactly perform as the Sumerians suggest (a mixture of barley seeds from all parts of the seed head seem to have been used).

The kush and double-kush can therefore be defined as the Sumerians suggested and, although the unit will vary slightly from experiment to experiment, on average it remains quite accurate.

The Time–Distance Relationship

Having previously established that the length of the Megalithic Yard, a unit in use in the far west of Europe before and contemporaneously with the kush, had been ascertained by a combination of astronomy and geometry, we wondered if the kush had been proven in a similar fashion. The Megalithic people had swung a pendulum whilst observing the planet Venus as it dropped towards the horizon as an evening star.

We applied the same technique. We assumed that the Sumerians had created a braced wooden structure that could be set to match the angle of Venus as it fell towards the horizon. The 'window' of the structure would occupy 1° of the horizon, from the point of reference of the viewer. If a pendulum was swung during the passage of Venus through the window and was expected to maintain 120 periods or 240 beats during Venus' passage, the resultant pendulum would be 99.8cm in length, allowing for acceleration due to gravity in Sumer.

There is nothing here that would have been unknown to the Sumerian priests. The passage of Venus across $\frac{1}{360}$ of the horizon represented that period of time known to the Sumerians as the gesh. They would have known that there should be 120 Sumerian seconds of time during 1 gesh (240 modern seconds). The resulting length of the pendulum achieved is so close to achieving a double-kush, matching the half-kush of the Gudea statues, that we fail to believe this is in any way a coincidence.

Put simply, the double-kush is derived from what is known as a seconds pendulum, because it swings in one second of time. The seconds pendulum is a device that was much studied during the 18th and 19th centuries in Europe and it very nearly became the basis of the metric system.

Why Use the Planet Venus?

One of the great difficulties about the seconds pendulum and the reason its length did not ultimately become the linear basis of the metric system lies in the fact that it is somewhat difficult to define. We have seen that the second of time is derived from a slightly hypothetical lunar synodic period of 30 days. Clocks in the 18th century were not particularly accurate and those devising the metric system were worried that there would be some variance if the unit was checked in different places, using different clocks.

The turning Earth represents a very accurate clock, but it may have occurred to the French academicians that there was no way of checking the seconds pendulum against the Sun or stars. The reasons are somewhat complex but important to understand and have to do with the difference between the solar day and the sidereal day. During a mean solar day, which varies slightly from day to day, there are 86,400 modern seconds of time. However, because of the slight fluctuations in the length of the solar day it is not possible to use the Sun against a known geometric background to set the seconds pendulum, simply because the length of the second would vary from day to day. A star is no use either, because the star or sidereal day is not as long as the solar day. If a star were checked against geometry, the second of time would be short and so would the achieved pendulum length.

The only celestial body that comes close to allowing an accurate assessment of the seconds pendulum is the planet Venus when, as an evening star, it moves rapidly away from the Sun. The fact that Venus is moving forward with the turning sky but also appears to be moving rapidly within the zodiac in a counterclockwise direction effectively lengthens the amount of time it would take to cross 1° of the horizon in comparison with an ordinary star. This would lead to a second of time that would actually be 1.002 seconds in length, which is $^2/_{1000}$ too long. However, it is as close as can be established through any naked-eye celestial observation. What matters about it is that the clock is accurate with itself. In other words, the result will always remain the same and the basic unit of length can be checked at any time when Venus is behaving in this way.

If one assumes that, to the observer, the last swing of the pendulum begins when Venus is still in the gap but ends when it has left the gap, we arrive at a unit of length of 99.8cm for the pendulum, assuming 120 periods. This is *exactly* the length of the double-kush inferred from the Gudea statues.

Of course it might be argued that, had the Sumerians simply used a star for their observations, they would still have ended up with a uniform unit of time. Though it would be shorter than a true second, the true second being $^1/_{60}$ of $^1/_{60}$ of $^1/_{360}$ of 30 mean solar days. It might be further suggested that stars would be more convenient for the purpose and could be checked on any night, rather than at the specific times Venus was available and behaving as required. Using a star for this purpose, the second would have actually been 0.997 of a true second and the double-kush would have been less than 99cm in length. We contend, and will show, that there are surprising but valid reasons why this could not be allowed to be the case.

The basis of all Sumerian linear measures was therefore intended to be as follows:

1 se = 1 barley seed = 0.2772cm

6 se = 1 shu-si or finger = 1.664cm

180 se = 1 kush or barley cubit = 49.94cm

360 se = 1 double-kush or double-barley-cubit = 99.88cm

Units of Mass

It is known that the Sumerians had a basic unit of weight or mass, known as the mana. It is further suggested that this weight was about ½ kilo. Surviving examples of the mana show it to have actually been in the range from 483 to 518 grams. We suggest that its true weight was intended to be 498.2 grams, well within the range of evidence available and more or less midway between the two extremes. More to the point, the double-mana, which we also contend was the original unit of weight, was intended to weigh 996.4 grams.

The Contentious Cube

It was not lost on early investigators into the Sumerian system of weights and measures that there appears to be a direct relationship between the basic unit of length and the basic units of weight and volume. Modern experts tend to repudiate the notion that the Sumerians had established weight and volume units by making a cube with sides ⅕ of a kush and then filling such a cube with water. The amount of water contained by such a cube would be the volume unit and the weight of the water the basic weight unit.

Despite the protestations of modern experts, there is a direct relationship between Sumerian units of length, weight and volume. These relationships are obvious and quite clearly intentional. They *can be* created using a ⅕ kush cube, and the most plausible explanation for their existence is that they were so created. However, all the arguments in the world will not satisfy those who simply seem to repudiate these facts as a matter of 'faith'.

Part of the problem could be one of incredulity. It is our contention that the original mana was the double-mana, and that it was established from a cube with sides ⅒ the length of the double-kush. We have to bear in mind that the double-kush is almost exactly a metre in length and that those creating the metric system at the end of the 18th century created the kilo by way of a cube with sides ¹⁄₁₀ of a metre in length. *In other words, the basis of the metric system is as good as identical to the basis of the Sumerian system.*

It seems to be the case that there was and perhaps remains, especially amongst the French, a great deal of embarrassment in the fact that there is nothing remotely new about the metric system as it was first envisaged at the end of the 18th century, and that it is actually many thousands of years old. Livio C. Stecchini suggested that scientists simply cannot accept that the Sumerians were this bright. If that is the case, then our further discoveries are going to send them into paroxysms of indignation and rage.

The Unit of Weight or Mass

The mana, the basic unit of weight in the Sumerian system, is observed to be around ½ kilogram. It is our assertion that the original unit of weight was a double-mana, just as surely as the original unit of length was the double-kush. It was perhaps for practical purposes that the mana found in Sumerian archaeological sites was used. The proof of our assertion lies in the fact that the Sumerian sila, the basic unit of volume, is one litre. Only the sila retained its original double value in daily use, or in terms of what has been discovered on archaeological sites.

The se or barley grain was used not simply for units of length. It was also part of the weight-measuring system. The Sumerians said there were 10,800 barley grains to a mana. If the mana is half the weight of water that would fit in a cube with sides of 9.988cm, it should weigh 498 grams. This means that each barley grain should weigh 0.046 grams. Our own investigations show this to be a near-perfect weight for an average barley seed and the fact is also borne out by the independent weighing of barley seeds from the British 1979 crop. Our average weight for a barley seed was 0.0465 grams, and that from the 1979 crop was 0.045 grams.

We now have direct and verifiable proof that the Sumerians did in fact use barley seeds for both linear size and weight. There is also additional proof here that the original unit of weight was the double mana, which would contain 21,600 barley grains. 21,600 is 360×60, which is entirely in accord with Sumerian mathematical practices.

It can therefore be demonstrated that there are two independent ways of creating and verifying the Sumerian system of length and weight measurement. It can commence with a seconds pendulum, derived from the movements of the planet Venus, and then become a unit of weight via water in a cube with sides $\frac{1}{10}$ that of the double-kush. Conversely it can be a linear unit based on the size of barley grains and a weight unit based on the weight of barley seeds.

Nobody could doubt that this is an ingenious system, but it is far from being the end of the story.

The Mass of the Earth

Seen in modern terms, the mass of the Earth is $5.976×10^{24}$ kilograms. If this figure were to be $6×10^{24}$ units, then each unit would have a mass of 996 grams. This is precisely the weight of a double-mana that is created from a cube with sides $\frac{1}{10}$ of a double-kush. To turn this on its head, the mass of the Earth is equal to 6,000,000,000,000,000,000,000,000 ($6×10^{24}$) double-mana. Could this possibly be a coincidence? Of course it could. Almost anything *could be* a coincidence but, bearing in mind the fascination of the Sumerians for the number 60 and that their whole counting system was based upon it, rather we might ask is this *likely* to be a coincidence? Perhaps even more peculiar is the realization that this system allows for an understanding of the mass of the Earth in terms of barley seeds. The mass of the Earth is the same as the accumulated mass of $1.296×10^{29}$ barley seeds.

The Implications

The Sumerians used an integrated system of measurements that was verifiable in two separate and distinct ways, either via the size and weight of barley seeds or by way of a basic unit of length derived from the passage of time. The modern metric system of measurements, wonderful though it might be, falls short of what the Sumerian system achieves in a couple of ways. Time is still measured using a base-60 counting system, with 60 seconds to the minute and 60 minutes to the hour. This can never mesh perfectly with a metric system, which by implication must be a base-10 system. We have also demonstrated that geometry was part of the intrinsic whole and this too operates on a base-60 system, which metrics do not.

In a day-to-day sense this probably does not matter because we are generally used to flipping from the metric to a sexagesimal system. All the same, there is something deeply ingenious about the Sumerian model and, had it been adopted in its entirety, it would have been no less accurate or useful than the metric system, a partial system, turned out to be.

Those who instigated the metric system of measurement at the end of the 18th century in France originally discussed the possibility of using the length of a seconds pendulum as the basic unit of linear length. They decided on a different course of action only because it was difficult during this stage of scientific advancement to know exactly what a second of time actually was. Instead, they carefully measured a quadrant of the Earth, from the North Pole to the equator, and divided the result into 10,000,000 units. One of these units became the metre. It was reasoned that, if ever the sample metres were lost or damaged, they could be recreated because the size of the Earth would not alter.

Is this more accurate than the Sumerian system? Probably, though the French scientists, accurate as they were, didn't get their metre quite right with the size of the Earth. The metre as defined from the quadrant of the Earth should actually be 1.00025m in length. It doesn't matter in the slightest now, because the metre is presently ascertained with reference to a much more accurate light-based system.

What remains extremely interesting is how close to the Sumerian double-cubit (or double-kush) the metre turned out to be. There seems to be a degree of serendipity involved, but we cannot be certain how much of a part the seconds pendulum played in the ultimate decision. When the English were discussing new units of measurement at the same time as the metric system was being defined, they still talked about verifying their basic unit with reference to a seconds pendulum. Perhaps the French simply opted for a division of the quadrant of the Earth that would offer them a basic unit of length that they *knew* to be close to that of the seconds pendulum. After all, the two lengths are only about 1mm different.

Whatever the reason, the French system did offer us a *clue* as to the original scope of the Sumerian system. It simply *must* have puzzled some experts when it was realized that the mass of the Earth turned out to be 5.976×10^{24} kilograms, because this is so close to being a recognizable integer number. Doubtless it was put down to a peculiar coincidence. We contend that it was nothing of the sort. By opting for a unit that was so close to the Sumerian double-kush, which had been 'tuned' to the mass of the Earth, the metre and the kilogram derived from it could not have failed to so nearly divide the mass of the Earth in this remarkable way. But there is another apparent coincidence, the implications of which might be even more shocking.

The Speed of Light

The speed of light is 299,792,456 metres per second. Once again, it cannot have failed to surprise whoever arrived at this figure to see how closely light was to making a neat integer number when expressed in the metric system. Of course this must be a coincidence, particularly since 300,000,000 metres per second does not have any particular significance to anything. However, 300,000,000 double-kush is significant because, when expressed simply as kush, we get 600,000,000 kush, another very Sumerian-looking number.

The actual number of kush to the speed of light in one second is 600,305,278, which is accurate to a round 600,000,000 to within 1 part in 2,000. In metres the accuracy against a round 300,000,000 metres per second is 1 part in 1,450. An absolutely accurate linear measurement to split light into 600,000,000 units per second would be 99.93cm in length. No matter how absurd it might seem to suggest that the Sumerian system might have been calibrated to take light speed into account, it remains a fact that the kush is 99.99 per cent accurate when it comes to expressing the speed of light as 600,000,000 kush per second. The fact that the metre is almost as accurate at expressing the speed of light as being 300,000,000 metres per second is merely a reflection of how close the metre is to the Sumerian double-kush.

Conclusion

We are well aware that experts will nit-pick to prove that what we are saying is clearly nonsensical. There is no guesswork involved here. We took the length of the half-kush shown on the Gudea statues as our starting point. These were carefully carved into extremely hard stone and they have not altered with the passing of the centuries. While it might be argued that the Gudea statues represent nothing more than the half-kush, as it happened to be at that time, we believe that such a suggestion doesn't really stand up to scrutiny. The Gudea statue measure performs flawlessly when, as the double-kush, it is checked against the passage of Venus across one degree of the sky. The possibility of this happening by chance is so remote as to be virtually impossible.

We showed that the method used for creating both length and weight measures the Sumerians used is still quite valid and that there is nothing hypothetical about the barley grains to which they referred. Arguments about the different nature of barley seeds used in Sumerian times, as against modern ones, are also irrelevant. The fact is that both our samples and those from the 1979 British crop did what the Sumerians said they would.

While it is surprising to realize that the basic unit of weight in the Sumerian system was carefully calibrated as a known and logical component of the mass of the Earth, the figures speak for themselves. They are correct when set against the weight of water in a cube with sides $\frac{1}{10}$ of a double-kush (the kush derived from the measurements of the Gudea statues). There are only two possibilities: whoever invented the system was aware of the mass of the Earth, or the whole thing is an most outrageous coincidence. How those creating the system could have known the mass of the Earth is a puzzle, but it is a *separate* puzzle because we maintain it is clear that they did.

We further realize that suggesting that the speed of light might have lain at the heart of this system is going to infuriate historians. Once again the figures speak for themselves. Either what we have observed is a genuine reflection of the knowledge of those who created the system, or it is a random chance event. No figures have been massaged, and the linear unit in question is that taken from the half-kush on the Gudea statues.

What we find is a holistic measuring system with a decimal/sexagesimal base that measures time, distance, volume and mass, using the same figures throughout. It can be created from barley seeds or as a fragment of time when measured with a pendulum.

It is possible that people will tell us that we have mixed up measurements and made much out of units that are not standardized. They will certainly say that the Sumerians were incapable of cubing any unit, and therefore the sila is not the volume of water in a $\frac{1}{5}$ cubit cube, or that the mana is not the weight of that water. However, many mana weights have been found. These vary from 495 grams to 518 grams. In our estimation the true figure is around 498 grams, arrived at by weighing the water held in a cube with sides ⅕ of a kush. We do not suggest that all agencies in Sumer and after always got it right.

Duncan J. Melville, Associate Professor of Mathematics at St Lawrence University in Canton, NY, runs a website on Old Babylonian and Sumerian weights and measures. He does not try to achieve *absolute* figures, but he says the kush is 'about' half a metre. He says the mana is about half a kilogram and that the sila is about one litre. He quotes these figures because they are generally considered to be correct.

Independent proof of the size of the kush is derived from the half-kush on the Gudea statues, which would place it somewhere around 49.94cm. This would make sense of the mana and the sila in its half form. However, there does seem to be some slight confusion, which may well be down to interpretation of texts, because either the mana was originally exactly twice the size stated or else the sila was exactly half the size stated.

The system as we believe it to have been has two tiers. It can be based either on time, which is turned into linear length and then made into volume and weight. Alternatively, something almost identical, though not quite so accurate, can be created from the size and weight of barley seeds.

The Sumerian System, at least in its intended form, was a decimal/ sexagesimal system of great power and elegance. It encompassed the passage of time, length, volume, mass and area. It was a system with two points of entry, either through the passage of time or through the size and weight of a barley seed. In both systems the results were more or less identical. A feature of the system was its elegant geometry, which was the same geometry we still use today.

NOTES

1. Butler, Alan, *The Goddess, the Grail and the Lodge*, O Books, 2003

2. Knight, Christopher, and Butler, Alan, *Before the Pyramids*, Watkins Books, 2009

3. Butler, Alan, *The Bronze Age Computer Disc*, Quantum/Foulsham, 1999

4. Butler, Alan, *The Goddess, the Grail and the Lodge*, O Books, 2003

5. Trollope, Anthony, *Barchester Towers*, 1857, London, ch. 22

6. Knight, Christopher and Lomas, Robert, *The Hiram Key*, Century Books, 1996

7. Butler, Alan and Ritchie, John, *Rosslyn Revealed*, O Books, 2006

8. Sanderson, Meredith, *An Examination of Freemasonic Ritual*, Baskerville Press, London, p. 923

9. William Bond's information on the Goddess and Freemasonry can be viewed at: www.womanthouartgod.com/wmbondfreemasonry.php

10. Robinson, John J., *A Pilgrims Path*, M. Evans, 1993

INDEX

Page references in italic type relate to captions.

A

Acre 156
Adams, John 122, 126
Age of Reason xiii, 4, 66
'All-Seeing Eye' 47–8, 48
American Civil War 171
American War of Independence 2, 52–3
Aphrodite 61
 see also Venus (goddess)
Aratus 65
Ark of the Covenant 142
Ashtoreth 139, 144–5
Astarte see Ashtoreth
astrology 64–80
 and astronomy 64–6
 for augury 4–5, 8, 66
 and Freemasonry 66–74
 and Washington DC xvi, 75–80
 see also zodiac
astronomy 64–80
 and astrology 64–6
 Earth's mass 203, 220
 Earth, Sun and Moon, relationship between 5–8, 6, 97, 129, 200–202, 209–10
 Earth and Venus, relationship between 74, 142, 195, 216–17
 and Freemasonry 66–74
 and Rosslyn Chapel 165–6
 and Washington DC xvi, 75–80

see also geometry; measurement systems; Shekinah; time measurement; zodiac
Athens 8–9
Athta see Ashtoreth

B

Baal 139
Bacon, Francis 120
Baldwin II, king of Jerusalem 154
Banneker, Benjamin 54
Barchester Towers (Trollope) 30–31
Bath 83, 102–3, 105, 127
Beautiful Virgin of the Third Degree 67, 68–71, 69
Bernard of Clairvaux 154–5, 158
Bernard of Ponthieu (or Thiron) 161
Bible 72–3, 125, 138–9
 Isaiah 72
 1 Kings 139
 Revelation 44–5
'Blazing Star' 73–4
Boyle, Robert 125
Bridget, St 30
Briggs, Isaac 54
Britain 50–52, 59–60
Brown, Dan 185
Bruce, James 141
Bryce, David 170
Bush, George W. 3

C

calendars see time measurement
Capitol (Washington DC) 1–2, 11, 75, 76

INDEX